It's a Sardine's Life for Me

A MEMOIR OF THE SCOTTISH RITE DORMITORY
AT THE UNIVERSITY OF TEXAS AT AUSTIN

Compiled and Edited by
Amie Stone King

NORTEX PRESS · NORTEX · Fort Worth, Texas

For Marillah, my SRD girl in training.

Copyright © 2007
By Amie Stone King
Published By NorTex Press
An Imprint of Wild Horse Media Group
P.O. Box 331779
Fort Worth, Texas 76163
1-817-344-7036
www.NorTexPress.com
1 2 3 4 5 6 7 8 9
ISBN-10: 1-68179-103-X
ISBN-13: 978-1-68179-103-6

Contents

Acknowledgments   xi
Foreword   xiii
Our Scottish Rite   xv

Having Fun! **1**
   Welcome Back   3
   Hello Darling   3
   Dancing, Dating, and Driving   4
   1939 Ford   5
   Animal House?   5
   Birthday Surprise   7
   A Date's Memories   7
   Ho-Hum!   8
   Kitchen Talk   10
   Biscuit War   10
   Eddie Rabbitt   11
   Gone With the Wind!   11
   It's ABSRD   11
   Me and Roommate Robin   12
   SRD Shows Hospitality; Navy Dances   13
   Tom Snyder Crush   14
   Beyond Our Wildest Dreams   14
   The SRD Auxiliary   15
   Curtain Wrap   17
   If I Ran SRD, I'd—   17
   Kappa Panties in Littlefield Fountain   18
   The Fijis   18
   Moon Walk   18
   Waiter Interview   19

Why We All Love SRD. 21
Spoiled Rotten Daughter 22
Too Well Hidden. 23
"The Ravin'" 23
To My Roommate 23
To the Boys Who Wait Tables. 24
An Ode to Inconvenience 24
Pizza Run 25

Memories From the Outside **27**
What an Outsider Thinks of SRD Girls 28
On the Wall at Lubbock Hall 28
April 9, 1920 28
A Letter from a Father 29
Scottish Rite Dorm Noting 50th Birthday 30
Sunshine Memories at SRD 31
Class of 2009 33
Ode de President 33
A Loving Witness 34
Recollections of Scottish Rite Dormitory 35
Panty Raid! 37
Mystery Man Gaily Strolls in SRD,
    Gladly Stampedes Out 37
A Palace Full of Princesses. 38
After Four Years. 40
Parents' Memories of SRD. 41
Pizza and a Cadillac 41
The SRD—An Outsider's Opinion. 42

A Memorable History. **45**
Masons Take First Steps to House Daughters
    at University of Texas. 46
Architecture Is Important 47
What's in a Name? 47
Dedication Services of New Scottish Rite Dormitory
    Are Held Thanksgiving Morning. 48
New Scottish Rite Dormitory Dedicated
    by Texas Masons 49
Arm Bands. 50

How Do You Like Staying in a Modern Dormitory?   51
Dear Santa Claus   52
Gifts to the Dormitory   53
Scottish Rite Girls Celebrate Raising of Flag
    from Mt. Vernon   53
Dorm Receives Colonial Clock   54
Scottish Rite Girls to Formulate System
    of Self Government.   55
Scottish Rite Dormitory.   55
SRD Seniors Honored at Tea   58
The Matrons   58
Sardine Dedicated to Mrs. Kauffman   60
A Tale of Two Bevos.   60
SRD To Hear Game   61
Famous Sayings   61
Annie   62
Rahs and Rants   63
On Dormitory Life   63
UT Seal Motto Is Translation of
    Mirabeau B. Lamar Statement   65
UT Column   66
Coy SRDines Hang Mistletoe to Catch Cadets
    at Formal.   67
News of D-Day Arrives on the Campus.   67
When Songs Are Sung.   69
If It's Listening You Are Wanting   70
SRD Committee Chosen to Study House Relations   70
Masonic Solons to be Honored.   71
Scottish Rite Dorm Feted by Masons   71
Smooth Operator   72
Coeds Contradict Phone Grumblings.   72
SRD Coeds: Fill in Blanks   75
Dorm Directors Bar Phone Survey   77
Stump Speakers Sift SA-SRD Situation   80
Lights in the Dark   81
SRD Will Be Real Cool   82
SRD Waiter Says Asked to Resign.   82
SRD Receives Bust of Masonic Leader   84
Is SRD Really a "Haunted House"?   85

Spirited Cooking. 86
Mary Frances Crosby 87
Interesting People. 87
Still Cookin'. 88
Wanted. 91
Alumnae Association and SRD Reunion 1990 92
Yesterday or Yesteryear? Chances Are
    Your Reunion's Near. 94
Scottish Rite Dormitory Celebrates
    75 Successful Years 94

Rules, Rules, Rules **99**
You Have To Be Mighty Smart— 100
Locked Out 100
Afternoon Tea and Celebrities 101
Family Style. 101
No Pants Allowed. 102
Fashion Forward. 102
Handbook for SRD Girls 103
The Witching Hour 104
Dating Protocol 104
UT Column 105
Kiss and Tell 105
Trays and Ice. 106
Follow the Rules, or Else! 106
Don't Mess with Patsy! 107

It's Personal **109**
Granny Brat. 110
Letters from Home 110
More Than Just "Housekeeping" 111
A Closing Thought 112
A Good Friend 112
SRD Girls Concerned Over Illness of "Dad" 112
UT Ex Ritter Returns for Austin Stockshow. 113
The Daily Dozen of a Sardine 114
My Time as a Waiter. 115
A Family Affair. 116

Beauty Is a Pinch 117
A Rosy Reward. 117
A Heartfelt Memory 118
Love and Support 118
SRD Exhibits Paintings 119
Daddy Was a Mason. 120
Waiters and Friends 120
A Family Tree. 121
A Conversation with Stella 121
More Than Just Waiters. 125
SRD Nips Hargrove by One Penetration 126
A Darkhorse Tale 127
Yes, Marillah, Daddy Was a Waiter. 127

How Far Will They Bend? **131**
The Stash 132
The Complete Guide to Perfect Ladyhood 133
Curfew 134
Ice Storm. 135
Laundry Cart Thrill Ride 136
In and Out. 136
Smooching. 137
The Sewing Project 137
The Physics Lesson. 138
Juanita 139
A Special Place. 140
Lost in Space 141
The "Pit". 142
The UT Column 142
Prim and Proper? 143
Man on the Hall. 143
"Main-*Tain*!-Ance Men". 144
What the Maintenance Man Saw 145

Girls Will Be Girls! **153**
And, Alice, Looking into the Past, Through
    the Looking Glass Was Surprised,
    Almost Unbelieving— 154
Patsy's Animals 155

Front Page News. 156
The Hand on the Hall 156
Some Statistics. 156
A List of Demands 157
SRD to Have First Dormitory Swimming Pool 158
Making a Splash. 160
UT Column 160
TV and Caviar 161
Caught in the Act 161
More Broken Bones 162
Bored Co-eds Bring Fame to SRD 162
Star Delights SRD Diners 164
Mrs. Fowler's Cleaning Frenzy 164
SNAKE!. 165
Pickles. 165
The SRD Mouse Trap 165
No Screaming on the Hall 166
Itty Bitty Living Space. 166
Dining, Biking, and the Long Kiss Goodnight 168
What a Place 168
The Sprinkler System 169
No Special Treatment 170
Dube's Dolls 170
TV Bonding 171
SRD Memories. 171
Chilling 172
Squirrel Interrupted 173
Things My Daughter Learned While at SRD... 174
UT Column 174
Butch 174
Keils' Wheelchair 175
Attic Anna. 176
Boo! 176
Just Being Girls? 176
Our Neighbors 178
Top View. 180
Touches of Home 180
A Continued Connection 181
We Won't Forget... 181

Homage to My Friends 182
Mrs. 182
Mourning the Loss 183
5th Victim Claimed, 4 UT Coeds Die in Wreck 183
Scottish Rite Dormitory Memorial 184
A Wedding Story 185
Food and Water 187
A Memorable Place 187
Residents find Scottish Rite Desserts Irresistible 189
Room Service 189
Tornado! 190
Holidays and Special Events 190
Girls Deck Dorms in Holiday Décor 191
Egg Dye Dilemma 192
The Secret 193
On Top of the World 194
No Room in the Inn 194
The UT Tower 195
And the Winner Is... 200
Waiters Give Corsage Prize 200
History, Furniture, and Character 201
Elevators, Phones, and Don't Go There! 201
Driving School 202
Bing Crosby 202
Current Thoughts About SRD 203
A Lesson by Candlelight 204

Farewell 206
Afterword 207

Acknowledgments

Thank you to everyone (past and present residents, past and present employees, past and present waiters, family, friends, and strangers) who submitted stories, answered my questions, gave me research support, and willingly shared their thoughts about SRD. This book would not have been possible without you!

To my mother, Annette, goes an enormous thank you for her tireless help editing all the stories, for sharing in my excitement about this project, and encouraging me all the way. And a great deal of gratitude to my father, Frankie, who made it possible for me to live at SRD. Thank you for that wonderful gift and thank you to the Masons who built this grand establishment.

Finally, thank you to my husband, Matt, past SRD waiter, wonderful supporter, and expert document formatter.

Foreword

As I read this book, again and again I recognized my own experiences—not just from my own era of the sixties, but from the earliest times and the latest. The dress restrictions that led us to walk through the living room with a raincoat hiding our tennis shorts, the formal, sit-down lunches with one of us presiding at each table as hostess, the sign-out sheets and curfews have all been relaxed over time. But like a familiar character in a favorite novel, SRD is always itself in these pages, whether the memory comes from the 1920s or the 21st century.

How can a dorm evoke such specificity of memory over such a stretch of time?

Maybe it's the place itself, so gracious in its pillars and grounds. Official university dormitories, always constructed with a concern for making the taxpayer's dollars stretch, would never have been designed with a greenhouse for the cut flowers that graced the formal dining room. Even when flowers and tablecloths disappeared, the fact that SRD was built to accommodate them is always present in the spirit of the place. It was intended as a home for ladies—and the very building seemed to expect a certain behavior of us.

Or maybe the formality of architecture and expected behavior offered constant temptations for imaginative rule-breaking, mostly of a harmless kind. (Was I really breaking the "no electrical appliances for cooking" rule when I bent my metal goose-neck study lamp down close enough to toast my pop tart?) Breaking a rule was an event—and years later, it's the events that are memorable.

But what shines through all the stories of pranks and waiters and CCBs and the pit is the depth of the friendships that were formed at SRD. While it's not unusual to form lasting attachments during this time of life, SRD seemed to have a greater proportion of girls with whom you would want to form friendships.

I have a theory about this, which I formed when I lived at SRD. On Tuesdays and Thursdays, I would arise at 4 A.M. and be let out by the night watchman so that I could wait in front of the dorm to be picked up for my early morning work at a biology lab. As I sat on the cold stone bench in front of the darkened dorm, I would be aware of the sleeping girls inside that warm, protective place, built by Masonic fathers for their daughters. All I knew about Masons was that my father and grandfather and many early founders of our country were Masons; that they had strong values; and that one of those values was a deep caring for the people for whom they were responsible. That meant that every girl in the Scottish Rite Dormitory was connected, even if indirectly, to an ethic of caring. We were connected to a value that is at the heart of the cultivation of friendship over time.

Whether or not my theory is true, what is certainly true is that SRD fostered a culture of friendship and that many of those friendships have lasted through lifetimes. This book reminds us how grateful we are for the friends we found there.

—BETTY SUE MARABLE FLOWERS
1965-67

Our Scottish Rite

Oh Scottish-Rite, our Scottish Rite
For you your girls would always fight,
We come from city, cot and hall
In answer to fair learning's call.

The Masons all so kind are good
Have done for us more than they should,
A home more beautiful and fair
No girl could wish nor ever care.

Our matrons are the finest yet,
Our food is wholesome, you can bet;
We have fair halls to greet our beaux
And lovely closets for our clothes.

Our vanities of girlish lure
Were made our beauty to insure.
And comforts all that one could wish
Delight the even home-sick fish.

We honor you for what you've done,
And hope to merit it—just some,
We'll study hard and make you proud
Or else we'll wish we wore a shroud.

So welcome to your work so fair
And know your daughters love and care,
We'll bring renown to your lov'd name
And spread abroad the Masonic fame.

—Floy Jane Norwood
    Freshman, Scottish-Rite Dormitory, 1922
    The Annual Sardine, Volume 1, #1 1922-1923

Welcome Back

(To the tune of the theme from Welcome Back Kotter)

Welcome here. Your fun times have just begun.
Welcome here. You're at the school rated number one.
It's big and it's strange and it's new to you,
But it's yours and it's home, you'll find that's true.
We're in this together (Echo: We're in this together)
Through clear or rainy weather. (Clear or rainy weather)
You've worried a lot, but you've found your spot in SRD,
SRD, SRD, SRD.

Welcome back. Exams were your ticket out.
Welcome back, to the same old place you laughed about.
The faces have changed since you've been around.
Your dreams are the same but they've turned around.
Who'd have thought they'd lead ya (Who'd have thought
    they'd lead ya)
Right here where we need ya? (Right here where we need ya?)
We tease it a lot, but SRD's still our spot
Welcome back, welcome back, welcome back, welcome back.

Hello Darling

(To the tune of *Hello Dolly*)

Well, hello Darling
You're Some Real Darlings
It's so nice to have you where you belong.
You're lookin' great Darling
We could hardly wait Darling
Now it's time to play and eat all night long.
Well, the Coke's flowing
And the corn's popping
And the scales are tipping from our midnight snacks.
But, that's okay, Darlings
The men love you anyway, Darlings.
They will never stay away,
We're so glad you're here to stay,
Please don't leave us 'till next May,
We're so glad you're here in SRD!
—ADVISOR CREATED SONGS, 1976–1977

Dancing, Dating, and Driving

I lived on the second floor directly over the front door in the early 1930s, which was during the deep Depression. Money was tight for everyone. My mother sold some land for $400, and that put me through UT for two years. Living in the dorm was $75 per month. My uncle was a Mason, and he helped me get into SRD, which at the time was thought of as the best place to stay at UT. The matrons and all the employees at SRD were very protective of the residents. One matron, I think her name was Ms. Cooke, was elderly and would pretend she couldn't hear so the boys would have to get really close to say the girl's name. This way she could smell their breath and see if they had been drinking.

The phone system at SRD left something to be desired. There were only three phones per floor and a little buzzer would go off in your room when you received a call. You never knew if it was for you or your roommate, and whichever one went running for it, it would be for the other. Sometimes we even went to other floors when all of our phones were busy, and this was most of the time. It was such a chore to get a line into SRD that some fraternities used it as part of their initiation. The boys had to call until they got a line into SRD, which could take 30–40 minutes.

From my window you could see all the girls who smoked lined up, after dinner, in front of SRD for their last smokes of the evening.

A football player once told me that he came to UT with only two pair of khaki pants. This was his reason for not being able to attend dances at SRD or UT. SRD's weekly dances were a great aid to our social life as well as our morale, but there was no beauty shop near campus so a fellow resident solved that problem by offering a pin curl service for 25 cents per girl. Even though the dances gave us time with young men, we had plenty of dates as well. One boy I went out with a few times told me he was dating me solely to be invited to the Friday night dances at SRD!

Coke dates on the drag were also very popular. You ordered one bottle and two straws for 5 cents, and that was the date.

Still, the majority of our day trips consisted of visiting a local ranch possibly named Dillingworth. Our dates would rent a Ford Roadster with a jump seat for $5 per night plus gasoline. Each boy brought a blanket, and the four of us would hop in and go. The owner was an obliging man who patrolled the grounds on horseback. He would announce when there was 30 minutes before SRD's curfew, and then the fun began! In order to save gas the drivers would all drive backwards (maybe 20 miles) to erase mileage. Of all the laughing and yelling I never remember any accidents.

—GENEVIEVE STERNS COX
1931–1933

1939 Ford

One of the most exciting things from my time at SRD is that I had a car which they let me keep in one of the garages. My 1939 Ford originally belonged to my grandmother who raised me, kind of.

My whole family lived in a duplex. I lived on the side with my grandmother and my parents and sister lived on the other side. It was wartime so gas was rationed. Luckily, my parents had the same kind of car. They pooled their fuel tickets so I would have enough gas to get to school in Austin from Kennedy.

Having that car was so much fun, but we all quickly became mechanics, learned how to change tires, etc. It was fun to drive in Austin then. We would all pile in and go to Barton Springs and sometimes we would even drive to Dirty Martins, which was about 200 yards from the dorm.

—JERRY COCHRAN MOORE
1944–1945

Animal House?

I remember the mass of girls moving into SRD in 1976 when I entered the dorm and was greeted by advisors wearing "Some Real Darling" T-shirts. These girls helped carry luggage and dorm gear to our rooms, gave advice and made us feel welcome. Candy Andrews helped me move in. As it turned out, she had relatives from my hometown. Candy and I became good friends and later, fellow Resident Assistants. The next year I wore an SRD advisor shirt of my own. Our theme was "Spoiled Rotten Daughters."

The advisor skit night and waiter talent show was lots of fun. The advisors came up with skits and songs. One time the advisors did a skit portraying the waiters to the tune of *Greased Lightning*.

And speaking of waiters, who could forget those wonderful sit-down meals! About 15 minutes before meals the stairwells would start filling up. We always tried to get there early so we could get to our favorite table. As the year progressed, our "table families" would develop. Each girl had her favorite waiter or two!

Then there were special meals when the Board of Directors would visit. This was certainly a time when we could count on great food and CCBs! As advisors and R.A.s, we were expected to escort the "little old gentlemen" who were on the board. It was kind of like entertaining your grandfather. Does anyone remember the little lady who came with her husband to the board meetings and dinners? She was really tiny and loved to flirt with the waiters!

Since we're talking about eating at SRD, might as well mention the food fight.*

I think it was February of 1978. Each year the advisors and waiters "traded places." Advisors would wait tables, and the guys would sit at one of their tables and enjoy being served. This particular year, someone threw something (probably a roll) and before you knew it everything cut loose, salad, salad dressing—you name it. I honestly don't remember who started this, and I'm sure those who do will carry this secret with them forever. It was a real mess and the ladies were not very pleased. Needless to say, this was the last year for that role reversal!

—ANNA HOLMGREN
1976–1979

*"Once it escalated past the rolls I got under the table because I had on a suede top and didn't want that ruined."—Kathy Keils, 1976–1980

Candy Andrews who actually started the food fight had this to say in her defense:

> It was the Valentine's Day dinner the year I was President of the Advisors, and we were doing the traditional switch where the advisors served the dinner while the waiters sat to eat as guests. Someone told me it was traditional for the head table to start a friendly food fight—evidently that wasn't the case. I had no idea the food fight would be as big an issue as it became. I started the affair by dumping a plate of food into the headwaiter's lap. From there it escalated into a full-blown Animal House-esque food fight. It was such a mess that everyone involved stayed and cleaned the dining room so as not to make any extra work for the staff.

Birthday Surprise

On my birthday one year for a surprise, my friends had a cake made for me by the SRD kitchen staff. That night the dining hall was serving liver and onions with bacon, and I wasn't happy about having to eat at SRD and told my friends we were going to the Spanish Village instead. In order to make me stay they said, "Oh, no, we're eating here and we'll all give you our bacon." I begrudgingly stayed, and when they brought the cake out and surprised me, I almost burst into tears!

—MYRA LEE SUMMERS
1940–1942

A Date's Memories

No guys could go upstairs so Cynthia and her friends fixed me up and put me in the laundry basket and covered me with laundry and drove me up the elevator to the second floor and around the halls and then brought me back down. I never left the laundry cart the entire time.

In football in 1981 or '82 Texas was #1 in the nation. We

met in the Rec Room to watch as Arkansas beat Texas 42 to 7. It was terrible.

I spent many a night sitting in the office with Cynthia as she did her RA duties. I remember a men's restroom down the hall that is now a women's. It had UT décor from the wallpaper to the toilet lid.

I met my in-laws for the first time at SRD. They were sitting on the pink semi-circle couch. I was sweaty, had my chain around my neck, and was out of breath from riding my bike to the dorm.

When I came in to pick her up for a date, there were six phones. If you didn't know the number, you'd have to ask the RA.

We used to go on dates and if it was past 12:00 A.M., she had to come in the security door and show her ID. At that time the parents could choose 12:00 A.M., or 2:00 A.M., or nothing for you.

One night I was taking Cynthia home and near 27th and Speedway there was a fire hydrant lying in the road so I got out and picked it up and threw it in the back of the car. There happened to be a parking place right in front of Prather dorm where I lived. I got the fire hydrant out of the trunk and placed it on the curb by the parking space. The next day I went to class and when I got back, that space was still open because parking wasn't allowed beside a hydrant. I repeated this for maybe three or four weeks. One day I got back, and UT had painted a yellow curb there. In later years we'd return to UT for a visit, and the yellow curb among the other white curbs would be there for no reason.

—CHRIS HORSLEY
SRD husband

Ho-Hum!

Dear Jack, Of course I love you still,
Of course I'm being true,
You heard I had a date with Phil?
He can't compare with you!

And so you needn't have a fear,
Two two-time is a sin,
So don't you fret if you should hear,
I'm wearing Tommie's pin!

♦ ♦ ♦

I really must write that French,
And be a Study-Bug,
So you had best let someone else,
Escort you to the "drug."

Now let me see, page 21,
I'm proud of my will-power, . . .
Hello, no, Jim, I really can't,
Go with you to the "Tower."

Now what page was it? 21, . . .
My shoes are surely muddy, . . .
Oh heck, let's see a flicker, Jane,
I'm in no mood to study!

♦ ♦ ♦

We wear bright scarves upon our heads,
And "panda"* dolls are on our beds,
Our lingerie shows through thin shirts,
We have those new fan-pleated skirts.

Angora sweaters, pastel felts,
And saddle shoes, the widest belts,
The '39 Sardines are thus—
In '49 we'll laugh at us.

—*THE SARDINE*
Volume 17, 1939

*Andy Panda was a series of animated cartoon short subjects pro-
duced by Walter Lantz and released by Universal Pictures from 1939
to 1949. The titular character was an anthropomorphic cartoon
character, a cute panda. In the early version of the cartoon series,
Andy is a cub, whose father, Papa Panda, is frequently trying to
prove himself as a good role model. Later, Andy became a stand-
alone star in the vein of Mickey Mouse, and even acquired a Pluto-
like dog as a pet.

Kitchen Talk

Margarita is sitting in the employee dining area preparing to eat her lunch. I've left her with the voice recorder for a couple of minutes and asked her to tell me about her time at SRD. Apparently the waiters also want to get in on the action and are pestering her as she talks. Obviously she's one of the waiters' favorite kitchen staff because of her sense of humor.

"I'm a cook at Scottish Rite and just to make my story a little shorter, all these boys (waiters) are mean. They treat me bad, they talk bad about me, they argue with me all the time. You hear that already. They talking all that noise (waiters in the background). I always get treated bad.

"They argue with me everyday. All the waiters and dishwashers."

"We're buddies," a waiter interjects.

"We're buddies because the recorder's on. That guy just threw a paper at me. That's my whole story for right now. Hey, hey, I'm eating and Colin is throwing paper balls at me. Bye!"

"One day I was cooking and they wanted to throw me into the trash can. Colin did that. He also tried to put me through the dish machine. Then they wanted to throw me inside the sink in the kitchen, but that ain't nothing new. Well, this is the end of my story."

—Margarita Munoz
Kitchen Staff, 1996–present

Biscuit War

It's my first year as a waiter at SRD. We had a little biscuit war at one time. I struck a guy in the head with a hard wheat biscuit, I think, and he retaliated, and it was fun. We have a good time as waiters. I'm not in a fraternity, but we have our own little fraternity here as waiters. We cutup and have a good time. It's the greatest job in the world! (And you can say I said that.)

—Zach Hoerster
Waiter, 2006–present

Eddie Rabbitt

We lived in the "pit" which was a hallway down in the basement. Some other residents from Huntsville went to an Eddie Rabbit concert and decided it would be fun to sneak on the tour bus and see him. They got on the bus, hid behind a curtain and about Smithville, Texas, they popped out and said, "Surprise!" Much to their surprise Eddie Rabbit was not on the bus, but the band was, and they put the girls out on the side of the highway. Without too much concern, they hitch-hiked back into town but arrived at the dorm after curfew and could not get in. They came knocking on my window to see if I could let them in (since the "pit" windows were at ground level). Eventually they climbed over the pool fence and got in that way.

—BECKY PINEHURST SMITH
1978–1980

Gone With the Wind!

One year we had a party themed, "Come As Your Suppressed Desire." I remember that Becky was an angel because that was really suppressed, and I was a Southern Belle complete with hoop skirt and all. For some reason we stopped by a gas station on the drag, and when I got out of the car, my hoop skirt blew up over my head, and I couldn't get it back down. There was a lot of honking and carrying-on as people passed by on the drag.

—ELLEN WRIGHT MITCHELL
1978–1981
—BECKY PANKHURST SMITH
1978–1980

It's ABSRD
(To the tune of *Mame*)

VERSE 1

To think that we're just some rich ol' dames—it's abSRD!

To think that we're the ones to be blamed—it's abSRD!
We try and try to pretend that some day in our homes
    we will mop;
But, how can that ever be when we know we're
    the cream of the crop?
VERSE 2
To think that we'll follow the rules—it's abSRD!
And if we don't? Will we be called fools?—it's abSRD!
My hours, the showers; I tell you it's more than
    a person can stand!
With "flush" and rush and the hush, will we get us
    a hunk of a man?
VERSE 3
Still we can't leave this dorm of ours—
It's full of love and fresh-cut flowers—
SRD's home and it's welcome to you!
               —ADVISOR THEME
                Written by Paige Holton
                1975–1976

Me and Roommate Robin

When we filled out our applications for SRD in 1960, we were asked our nickname and when you arrived, that was the name on your door. Robin's name is actually Alice Margaret, but when we got to the dorm, Robin was the name on her door. Everyone from high school and before calls her Alice, and to everyone from SRD and later in her life she is Robin. SRD is where she officially became Robin.

All laundry had to have tags with your name.* Whatever went to the laundry was boiled, starched, and pressed. So we would take our personal laundry and anything else we didn't wish to be ironed on a nail and put through boiling water to a Laundromat over on Guadalupe. One day Robin and I were on our way to the Laundromat with our little laundry bags of personal laundry, and some bored Fiji's were on their porch yelling obscenities at us. One said, "Whacha got in the bag?" and Robin yelled back, "Dead babies!" and kept walking.

One sad memory is of the day when JFK was shot. I was

leaving the dorm to go pick up Robin at the art school, and we were going to the parade because he was coming through Austin. I heard about it when I went to pick her up and got her and then we came back to the dorm. The largest TV in the dorm was in the Rec Room, and it stayed on for hours that day. Linda Bird was at UT then and was a Zeta. The secret service rushed the house and got her and whisked her away. It was a sobering time especially because he had been on his way to Austin.

—SYLVIA HULSEY WEST
1960–1964

*Sylvia's daughter Leslie, who also lived at SRD, asked, "So when you threw your panties down in a raid, your name was in them?"

SRD Shows Hospitality; Navy Dances

Almost every night is Texas hospitality night at SRD, think the thirty V-12ers who walked in one night just to look around and get acquainted.

The boys really meant to get acquainted, for ten minutes later matrons were scouting the upstairs stairs halls for girls to change from pajamas and rolled-up hair.

"Come downstairs and dance," they urged. "There is a stag line, long enough to make you realize there is no manpower shortage on this campus."

The matrons were right, there was a stag line and there was Texas hospitality for the V-12ers who have been dancing at SRD almost every night since.

The Daily Texan, July 8, 1943, reprinted with permission.

The V-12 Navy College Training Program was designed to supplement the force of commissioned officers in the United States Navy during World War II. Between July 1, 1943, and June 30, 1946, over 125,000 men were enrolled in the V-12 program in 131 colleges and universities in the United States. V-12 participants were required to carry 17 credit hours and 9½ hours of physical training each week

Tom Snyder Crush

During the 1970s, Tom Snyder was a late night talk show host that came on TV after Johnny Carson. A friend of mine had a huge crush on him. One night while I was studying in the fifth floor study hall, she brought me a copy of *People* magazine that said he was temporarily living in a hotel in New York City.

Since Spring Formal was coming up I told her she should invite him as her date and tell him it was some big UT event. She decided that was a good idea and that she would even pay his travel expenses. We laughed so much we had to leave the study hall.

When we got to her room, she called the hotel where he was staying. I was laughing so hard I had to go into the closet and close the door because she didn't want to laugh on the phone. In a low voice I could hear her asking the hotel desk clerk for Tom Snyder's room. Mr. Snyder answered the phone. My friend chickened out and hung up on him. He had answered with such a loud and forceful hello it rendered her speechless. I told her she blew it with Tom Snyder, and I don't think she ever tried to contact him again. I find it hard to believe that we actually thought that he would come to SRD Spring formal anyway. I guess that is how a 19-year-old mind works.

—Anonymous
1972–1975

Beyond Our Wildest Dreams

Four giggling, chatting young teenage girls burst into the dorm. They couldn't believe they were actually on a movie set and that today they would be meeting numerous stars. Having wrangled my way onto the set as a fresh-out-of-drama-school-director-wannabe, I was almost as excited as they were.

When I arrived that morning, someone was there to greet me and give me instructions for my "observation" of Richard Linklater that day. I was told where to stand, how to act during filming, when I could and could not approach the actors, and most importantly I was not to speak to Mr. Linklater until the filming was over for the night.

Determined to keep my composure, I ventured onto the set. It was amazing what they had done to the dorm's living-room to change it into a Victorian era French restaurant. Strolling through the set, I ran into Mary, a grip whose daughter was my flute student. It was nice to have a familiar face behind the scenes with me.

Although during filming, the dorm was supposed to be able to "function" somewhat normally from a business standpoint. That did not happen.

Filming commenced, and I stood in the small space where I had been commanded to stay. It was tricky to keep out of everyone's way, especially the make-up ladies. Even though I was there primarily to watch, I was soon given charge of the group of young girls and any other SRD employee who wished to come on set. I escorted them in and out, told them where to stand and tried to keep quiet when it was needed. Anytime there was an issue with noise or someone standing in the way one of the crew chiefs would look over and glare at me like, "Do something!"

It was a long afternoon, but we were able to talk with Matthew McConahey and Skeet Ulrich and take pictures with them. Ethan Hawke was pretty untouchable although the teen group cornered him and managed a picture. Matt, my husband, even came after work to join the fray.

When the shoot ended around midnight, I finally had my chance to talk to Mr. Linklater. He patiently gave me some quick advice and then let me take a picture with him.

Since this time I have worked on other movie sets, and I have to say that the only way to go is being a guest on the set and having the film made at SRD!

—Amie Stone King
1993–1997

The SRD Auxiliary

In view of the fact that some of the girls in the dormitory seem to be unaware of SRD's auxiliary for boys, *The Sardine* takes this opportunity to give them information concerning the organization.

One date with an SRD girl qualifies a boy for membership, provided he returns her safely home on time. It is our estimation that 75 percent of the boys on the campus are members of the auxiliary. In order to remain a member throughout the year, more strenuous qualifications must be met, but few of the members have any difficulty with them.

The president of the auxiliary is one who gives much of his time to promoting the cause of SRD—Herman Wright (much to Alice Arnold's approval). The parlor crew includes Wroe Owens, Bill Sprouge, Willard Bumpass, Searcy Ferguson, and Dause Bibby.

Some of the members have been spoken for, but there is still plenty of opportunity for any girl who is a willing worker. However, let us warn you that Harld Dyke, Tracy Ward, Nick Nichols, Alfred Mellinger, W. A. Johnson, Buster Johnson, Rutland Cole, Bill Hood, and R. Schley have "reserved," "keep off the grass," "apartment wanted," and similar signs attached to them which are of especial interest to Porter, Mann, Sanders, Stein, Fewell, Mueller, Dodds, Bennett, and Miller respectively.

Speaking of some of the other members, Jay Folbre doesn't distinguish one night from another; the auxiliary meets every night for him—he is most attentive to Frances Fitch. Those who rarely attend more than once a week—on Saturday night—are Ed Nesbitt, A. J. Ritter, Marshall Walker, James Haygood, Joe Renfroe, and Jack Clewis. And then there's a reason for Fred Sanders belonging to the organization, since he's so in love with a certain little brunette who lives here.

The following snacks of conversation heard at a meeting of the auxiliary will give you some idea of the work of the organization: Rosser Coke to Beth Duncan, "Let's shuffle off to Buffalo"; John McKay to Frances Stewart, "We're together night and day"; Minor Pitts to Mary Jane Mooney, "You'd keep twenty million people waiting, wouldn't you?"; Walter Moore to Frances Groseclose, "You're getting to be a habit with me"; L. M. Currey to Marjorie Boren, "Farewell to arms and serenades now that elections are over"; Theodore

Johnson to Mrs. Lawhorn, "I'm still without a sweetheart, and it's swimming season now" (may we suggest a sardine, Theodore?)

And so we close this brief resume of the SRD auxiliary for boys "till we meet again."

—*The Sardine*
Volume 11, 1933

Curtain Wrap

My favorite memory is when Candella Koomey* came bursting into our room late one night hiding from someone in hot pursuit, wrapped in a shower curtain. I never found out why that happened, and I thought it was so funny!

—Beth Baker Qualia
1974–1975

*Candella Koomey has no recollection of this event, but she says that it was when they lived in the "pit" and that someone had probably taken her clothes while she was in the shower.

If I Ran SRD, I'd—

Allow telephone calls until 8:30 Saturday night.
Permit after-dinner smoking.
Never combine grapefruit with spinach.
Have sausage for breakfast at least once a week.
Have Sunday breakfast at 8:30.
Pass a rule requiring all dormitory girls to speak to each other.
Give each girl a soundproof cell.
Install a sewing machine that would sew.
Double the number of telephones.
Serve three meals a day.
Answer long distance calls after 11 o'clock.
Lose my mind.

—*The Sardine*
Volume 13, 1935

Kappa Panties in Littlefield Fountain

In 1955 all the sorority pledges in the Scottish Rite Dormitory were discussing ways to "haze" their senior active sorority members. As president of the Kappa pledge class, I felt it my duty to do something more spectacular than, say, the Alpha Chi Omega pledges—not understanding, of course, that I had just pledged one of the most conservative groups on campus. I was very surprised to discover that some of my fellow Kappa pledges took my suggestions seriously, making a raid on the underwear drawers in the Kappa house. I crossed the campus, met my pledge sisters at the Littlefield Fountain— arms piled high with (white) undies—and waded right into the water.

—VIRGINIA NASH DEVENPORT 1955
Excerpt from *UT Memory Bank*

The Fijis

In 1978 or '79 it snowed, and I remember Lu Anne (Wisrodt) Freeman and I had a snowball fight with some Fijis.

I remember a Fiji pledge streaking through SRD two years. The first year he got through no problem, but the next year Mrs. Townes was at the dorm and the door was shut behind him. He was caught in someone's room on 1st West.

Also, I remember panty raids. There is a picture in the front of the UT yearbook of a Fiji panty raid that turned into the Fijis mooning SRD girls. The UT yearbook picture is of the SRD residents looking out of the west wing window and their gaze is decidedly downward.

—KATHY KEILS
1976-1980

Moon Walk

There was a guy here (a waiter), and he was arguing in the kitchen. He got mad, went to the back door of the kitchen and showed his butt as he left. He mooned all the ladies in the kitchen and everybody's face froze because they were in shock.

—MARGARITA MUNOZ
Kitchen Staff, 1997-present

Waiter Interview

Shannon Phillips 1980-82

Roy Ladel 1980-82

Amie: So, you were both waiters here at SRD?

Roy: When I wasn't studying, I was here working, and occasionally I would take a break from studies and come up here and try to help out. It was really hectic.

Shannon: We hardly saw Roy. He was always at the library studying.

Roy: Actually Shannon and I met at the library. We shared a carrel.

Shannon: Which library was that?

Roy: The Undergraduate Library, not the Perry Castaneda, the UGL.

Shannon: Oh, you even know the names of the libraries!

Amie: So when you were waiters . . .

Shannon: He actually never waited.

Roy: Yes, I was a dishwasher.

Amie: My husband was both. I married a waiter.

Shannon & Roy: Now who was your husband?

Amie: Matt King.

Roy: What years was he here?

Shannon: After us!

Roy: Oh, after us?

Amie: I was here from 1993-97.

Roy: Oh man, I'm feeling like 27 or something like that, you were here right after us, ha ha ha ha.

Shannon: We got here in 98.

Amie: Was it a good thing to be a dishwasher, or did you want to work up to being a waiter?

Roy: The dishwasher job was the preeminent position at the place because you dictated your schedule, you worked for 10 minutes a day, got all your meals, and had lots of free time for the rest of the day to study, which I did mostly, and then meet girls.

Shannon: Actually he got that wrong. He was a breakfast dishwasher, which means he was even lazier than the usual dishwasher.

Roy: It means you worked five minutes a day. THE best job here. THE one everyone wanted.

Shannon: Did you ever get up for breakfast?

Amie: Yeah, occasionally.

Shannon: Ah, okay, what was the best part?

Roy: What was the best part?

Amie: Mostly I ran down grabbed the bread and ran to the bus stop. What was the best part of being a waiter? Truthfully?

Shannon: The best part about being a waiter, well that answer is pretty obvious.

Amie: Well, it could be the food.

Shannon: Is my wife listening? Is my wife listening? It was the food, honey! For everyone else it was the WOMEN.

Amie: Did you marry a girl . . .

Shannon: I did marry a girl but not from here.

Roy: Nor did I, but I dated some SRD girls here and there.

Shannon: When he wasn't studying; and they went on dates to the library.

Roy: I'll tell you a happy memory; it was Ethel, one of the cooks.

Amie: Who's still here.

Roy: Ethel's smile. That was one of the more pleasant memories of SRD.

Shannon to Roy: Remember Momma, the woman that left right after we got here, chasing someone through the kitchen with a kitchen knife?

Amie: Goodness who was she chasing?

Shannon: Who knows but I'm sure he deserved it.

Amie: So did you do anything funny while you were a waiter?

Shannon: I remember that I trained the girls to finish very quickly. I had a table I would get out so fast. This other guy thought he was fast, and I'd be walking out while he was still serving. It was really kind of funny that the girls could be trained to eat faster.

Amie: You were a plate stealer!

Shannon: No, I really wasn't that bad about stealing plates. Just got them trained. But there was this one time when this girl came in late, and I was trying to be good about not stealing her plate. Apparently, she had some bad experience with guys taking things too quickly. When I took a bowl of food from the table, not her plate, she said, "No, I'm still using that." I turned around, took the bowl and put it on the table next to her and said, "When you can talk to me in a civil tone, I'll give it back to you," and walked off. You know she actually apologized to me.

Why We All Love SRD

- Because of the bells that wake us up every morning.
- Because of the nifty-looking late slips we sign when we're late.
- Because of the nice words of Mrs. Kauffman when one of us wears a hat down to lunch or dinner.
- Because of the excellent maid service.
- Because of the elite and ultra-modern ash trays in each room.
- Because of Emmagene Hale's bee-u-tiful voice.
- Because of the large amount of heat in the rooms in the winter.
- Because of the Irish potatoes with green confetti, the green peas, the green pea soup, the turnip greens, the green lettuce, and the other green stuff.
- Because of the inmates and their sunny smiles—their beaming faces—(and other trite expressions).
- Because of Majorie Williams and her "up-city" airs.
- Because of the dormitory Victrola and its new records.
- Because of the quietness, the peacefulness.
- Because of its nearness to campus.
- Because of the quiet hours.
- Because of the ease and quickness with which one's boyfriend can ring up to talk to one.
- Because of Jane Bland and her "cute little ways."
- Because of the people who snore on the sleeping porches.

- Because of the increased popularity one gets by thus signifying that one is the "dauh—tah of ah Mahson."
- And because—(censored).

—THE SARDINE, 1932

Spoiled Rotten Daughter

(To the tune of *Hello Mudda*)

Hello Mother—Hello Father,
This is your spoiled rotten daughter
Well it's fine here, could be better
Maybe 'cause I haven't gotten any letters.

We just had our Sunday dinner
And it looks like I won't be thinner.
Well the food here is fantastic
Only if the waiters wouldn't act so spastic.

Mom, I know this may sound crude
We saw the FIJIs in the nude.
Some were cute but, they're so naughty
And I've never seen such funny looking bodies.

Dad, I thought I'd better phone ya
Cause my roommate has pneumonia
And I hope this doesn't scare ya
I have heard there is a choker in the area.

Well, I got my class of science
But I couldn't get my finance.
My Professor's Hairi Krishna
He's a Commie and he always tries to kiss ya.

I have got a new advisor
And she surely seems much wiser
So I think this will be better
Mother, Father kindly disregard this letter.

—ADVISOR THEME SONGS
1977-1978

Too Well Hidden

One of my favorite SRD stories to tell is how the RAs and some of the waiters, who were working a deserted dorm one Easter/Spring break, were taking turns hiding Easter eggs and hunting for them until one egg went missing. The missing egg had been placed by one of the taller waiters in a globe of the lobby chandelier. No one noticed it, and he forgot where he put it.

That summer, what are the chances that I would be working the desk, at exactly the time the maintenance man was on a ladder cleaning the chandelier when I hear him exclaim . . . "What the heck? How did an egg get up here?" The heat from the bulb the hard boiled egg was resting against had dried up the egg, keeping it from rotting and burning all the way through the shell before it was found!

—CANDY ANDREWS
1975-1979

"The Ravin'"

While I pondered weak and weary
O'er some governmental theory,
Came a rapping and a tapping at my door—
Came a banging and a clanging at my door.
In a voice that even shook the floor
Came this visit to my door.
Alas! It is study never more.
Ah, never more.

To My Roommate

(Dedicated by the editor to her own, La Rue Simmons)

Within the walls of our small cell
As we on life's problems dwell,
There is no effort to be nize
As we others analyze.
There is no feeling of restraint

As we use the other's lip paint,
There is no feeling of regret
If we wear her hose when ours are wet.
There is no fond and soft, "Good Night;"
Instead, "When do you douse the light?"
This year is better, dear, because of you
Although at times things are askew.
Alas for her who never knows
The joy of wearing roommate's clothes!
                    —*THE SARDINE*
                 Volume 13, 1935

To the Boys Who Wait Tables

You've seen us in the early morning light—
The morning after a most hectic night.
You see our noses shiney,
And you hear our voices whiney
Ask for just another plate of food.
And, after getting it, we're often rude.

You see us in our ancient house-shoes.
You see us when we make no effort to amuse.
You'll thank us, boys, in later years
When on the scene your love appears.
The first sad shock of married lives—
The wife at seven—will be to you no big surprise.

An Ode to Inconvenience

Have you noticed my friends of the dorm.
That on cold days the room's never warm?
Haven't you found it as certain as fate
If you leave for a second, you're minus a date?
It never fails that while you're dressing,
You suddenly find the outfit needs pressing.
And always around the close of the week—
A lack of towels, a condition of which need I speak?

The candy, carried over from last Sunday's meal,
Has melted all over my new stocking heel.
I suppose as you read this you wonder why
I don't pick and leave SRD high and dry.
The answer's as plain as the nose on your face.
I'm honestly crazy about the place.

—*THE SARDINE*
Volume 13, 1935

Pizza Run

It was the end of the spring semester of 1972. My roommate and I, both freshmen living on Three East, were studying
for finals late one night when we decided that we could study
much better if we only had a pizza. In 1972 if you were inside the dorm after a certain time of night (I don't remember
what time that was), you could not leave; but because she and
I didn't have curfews, if we were already out we could get back
in. The more we talked about it the more we knew we needed
that pizza. The only option, we decided, was to sneak out
through a third floor window and climb down the fire escape.
And that's what we did! We got our pizza, got back inside and
best of all we didn't get caught! I don't remember what we
made on our finals!

—KAY KEILS POYNOR
1971-1973

Memories from the Outside

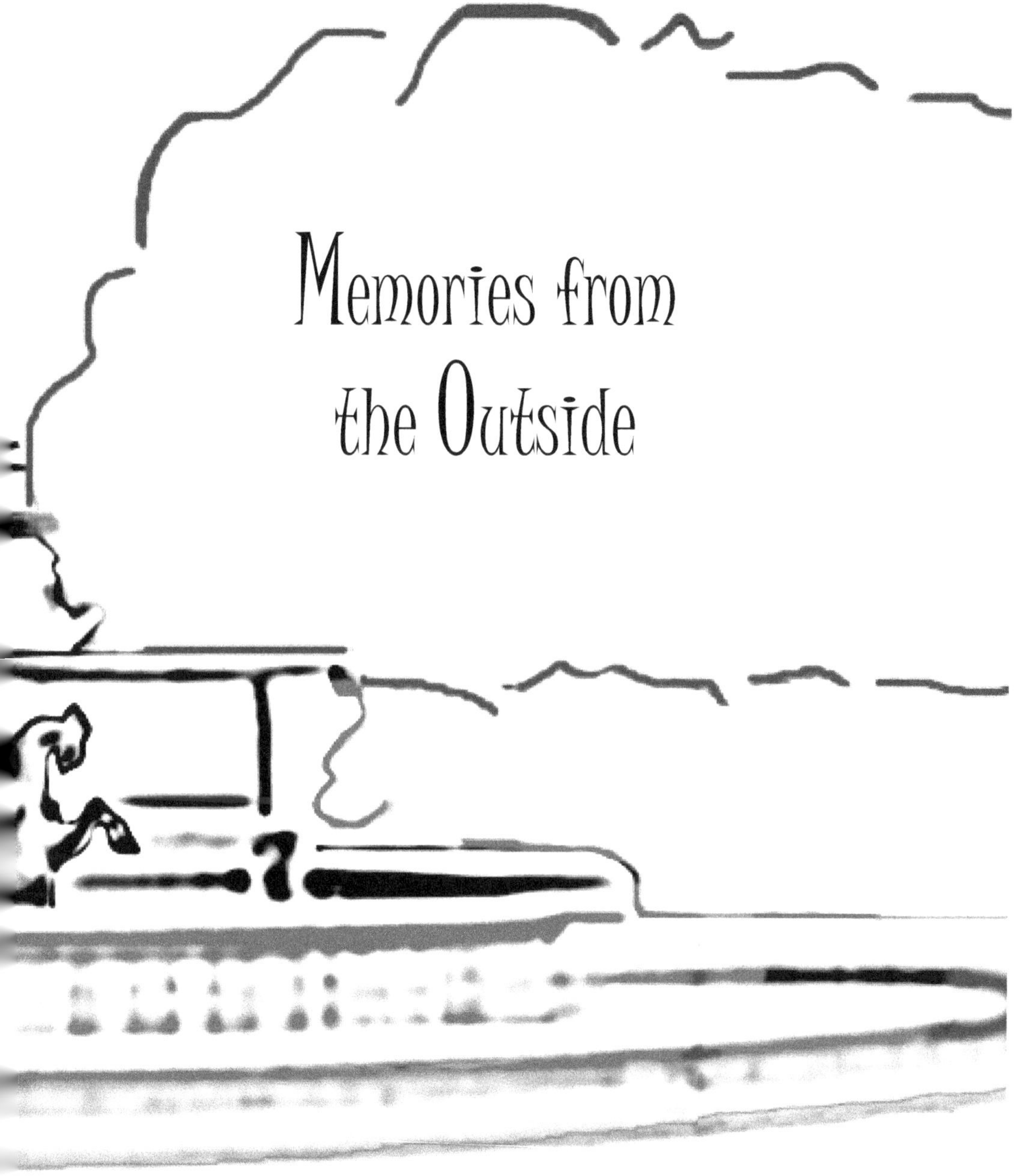

What an Outsider Thinks of SRD Girls

SRD has lots of girls,
Some have straight hair, some have curls.
Some are poor, some are wealthy,
Some are weak, some are healthy.
Some are short, some are tall,
Some are big, and some are small.
Some take care of just their looks,
Some just think about their books.
Some like to go out every night,
Some just like to get good and tight.
Some are sweet, and always pleasing,
Some are wenches, and always teasing.
Some are so awfully pretty,
That it makes me quite giddy.
But all in all, they do suit me,
The girls that live at SRD.
—"WINDY"
The Sardine, 1940

On the Wall at Lubbock Hall*

Across the way
Lies Scottish Rite.
I've busted my courses
And lost my sight.
—THE SARDINE, 1927

*Lubbock Hall was a men's dormitory next door to SRD at Austin Presbyterian Theological Seminary. The building was built with funds from a bequest of former governor Francis R. Lubbock.

April 9, 1920

Mr. T. H. Williams
Austin, Texas

My Dear Sir,

With further reference to your letter of April 1st;

I have decided to accept the proposition for lease of the entire plant and furniture of the Austin Presbyterian Theological Seminary, for the period of two years beginning August 21, 1920, at the rental of $6,600 for the first year and $7,200 for the second year; with the understanding that I will have the refusal to purchase this property at a price mutually agreed at any time prior to December 31, 1921, unless the Seminary desires to retain the property.

Judge James W. McClendon has been authorized to represent me in making the final arrangements regarding lease; and I have suggested to him that it will probably be better, if satisfactory to you, for the lease acceptance to stand in this shape until after the meeting of the General Board of Trustees, so that the lease agreement and purchase option (if granted) can be covered in one document. If, however, it is desirable to execute a formal lease agreement at once, Judge McClendon is authorized to act for me.

Assuring you of my appreciation of your courtesy in connections with these matters, and awaiting further (sic) advices with respect to final closing of the agreement, I am,

Sincerely Yours,
Sam P. Cochran
Sovereign Grand Inspector General
in Texas

A Letter from a Father

I have been intending to write a letter to the Scottish Rite staff for many years and will now use this opportunity to do so.

Our daughter stayed at the Scottish Rite Dorm for summer freshman orientation in 1993 and for the four years she attended UT.

My wife and I both attended UT and were therefore very pleased that our daughter chose to as well, but the idea of our "young" daughter alone on the UT campus and at the dorm was a bit much for me.

I called the dorm, probably about the time she was arriving for orientation, and talked to one of the staff. We talked briefly about the shuttle busses and I remember voicing some concern about them. The staff member on the other end of the line, in a very reassuring voice, said "We take very good care of our girls."

Those were prophetic words. Or said another way, truer words were never spoken as we learned very well over the next four years. I am so thankful that our daughter was able to room at the Scottish Rite Dorm for her UT years. It is the best investment we've ever made.

—Frankie Stone, SRD Father

Scottish Rite Dorm Noting 50th Birthday

Thanksgiving Day, 50 years ago, Scottish Rite Dormitory was formally dedicated.

Out for that occasion was then Gov. Pat M. Neff, University of Texas president Dr. Robert E. Vinson and the Ben Hur Shrine Band.

Saturday, with the Shrine Band again on hand, five decades of "sardines," as SRD residents are called, have been invited by the board, residents and staff to gather on the dormitory lawn, 210 W. 27th St., to celebrate SRD's golden anniversary. Parking will be available in the lots at 27th and University Ave., and 27th and Wichita St.

There will be plenty of reminiscing at the "Ole Fashun Ice Cream Social" because UT has changed considerably since the Hon. Samuel P. Cochran, 33rd degree, Sovereign Grand Inspector General in Texas of Scottish Rite Masons, envisioned a new residence hall on the campus which would provide suitable living quarters at a moderate price for the daughters of Master Masons.

But even though some former residents may be disconcerted by the freer language and lifestyles of today's students, they will be comforted to know many things are much the same at SRD as they were 50 years ago.

Although girls may now dine in halter tops and jeans, they still sit down to meals where fresh flowers grown in the dormitory greenhouse grace the tables.

On Sundays, white tablecloths come out, and girls still bring friends and dates for the traditionally scrumptious SRD noon meal.

On the other hand, former residents may well agree that the changes are good ones—that the Masonic governing board was wise to keep up with the times and, consequently, keep the dormitory full.

And because times do change, today's SRD girls have no hours if they are above first-semester freshman level. Neither do they rush out to the curb to smoke as they did in former days, or risk the possibility of a dormitory fire by extinguishing their cigarettes in the laundry chute when a housemother unexpectedly turns the corner.

Unlike their grandmothers and mothers (many of whom lived at SRD are legacies), girls may come and go as they please instead of being governed by rules stating, as they did in 1922, that "taking meals at a downtown restaurant is a violation of propriety" or that "no unchaperoned night automobile rides on country roads are allowed."

But despite the innovations—and there have been many, including a remodeling of rooms and the addition of an Olympic-size pool—SRD-ex's who return to celebrate will find that the growth of the University and the campus, hasn't marred the comfortable, homey atmosphere of the dormitory that has a long, happy tradition for taking care of its girls.

—CANDY LOWRY
The Daily Texan, October 18, 1972, reprinted with permission

Sunshine Memories at SRD

This southern belle was a foot taller than me, with porcelain skin, dusty brown hair and had a mischievous smile. Except for the smile, we had nothing else in common. I was short, brown and from the Far East. Being polar opposites made us a perfect pair.

Within a week of being in the same geology class, I remember her bringing me giant chocolate cookies and brownies. SRD had the best brownies! We have been friends ever since!

I had many "firsts" at SRD as I got to know this tall brunette. I remember my first egg painting party in her room and even though it's been 10 years since we graduated, we have still kept the tradition of painting eggs at her home with all our kids. She and I and other friends spread dozens of eggs on her dorm floor, some crinkle wrapped, some with elaborate miniature tropical sunsets, others that we hoped were perfect replicas out of Martha Stewart Easter magazines.

The SRD cafeteria was one of the best on the UT campus with an unlimited supply of lemonade and whoever heard of ice cream whenever you were in the mood for it!? She introduced me to a shy, dark-haired waiter once, and I remember thinking how lucky he was to be one of the very few guys allowed within the walls of the all-ladies dorm. Sure enough, she and Matt (the waiter) fell in love and were married after we graduated.

We all know how impossible it was to find parking on campus and driving from the suburbs to catch 8:00 A.M. classes was every student's nightmare. One semester, after circling the entire campus seven times, and not having my wallet with me, I wondered if I could just park as a friend of hers. Well, I had to try it. I was allowed to park at SRD which was prime real estate for parking since it was just two blocks from my classes at the chemistry building and the microbiology labs. That semester I had to spend six days a week at the microbiology labs and parking at SRD on several occasions was a great stress reducer!

I constantly found myself going back to SRD and enjoying privileges—that I would get by . . . uh, just asking? I remember walking up to the nice natured older woman who sat at the reception desk to see if I could sneak up to my friend's room and decompress between classes. I had had just 3 hours of sleep the night before and had 2 hours to kill before my late afternoon class. I was drooling in my last class and was sure to be snoring by my next if I did not catch a power nap. I was fast asleep in her recliner under a nice warm blanket when I was awoken by her laughter. The SRD staff had forgotten to mention that they had graciously let me into her room but she thought it was hilarious to find me snoring in her chair when she arrived home.

She and I plotted many crazy schemes at SRD, half of which materialized in between our endless study sessions in her dorm room. The four kids we have had in the past ten years have not slowed us down. She is now the "entertainment Godmother" to my children, always giving me the most creative last minute ideas for my parties. She is faster than a Google search for ANYTHING, and I have called her even before calling 911 on some occasions!

Even after all these years, I have gotten lost on the UT campus and Amie has come to my rescue, talking me through the roads as I walked in the rain to get to my GMAT classes. Of course we used SRD as a reference point.

—SARAH SIDDIQI
SRD Friend

Class of 2009

We love Scottish Rite Dorm. Our daughter Elizabeth lives here and I'm also signing up our younger daughter for the class of 2009. She's been to visit Elizabeth, and this is where she wants to go to school and live. It's beautiful, we feel secure, and she is very well taken care of. We don't have to worry about anything and when we come to visit we feel at home. She's got good food, a lovely room, and a lovely place. It's perfect.

—PAM MEDLIN
SRD Mother

Ode de President

Here is a poem by Prexy. He, being our next-door neighbor, we sent him over a huge cake on his birthday, and this rhymed narrative is his thanks. We think Prexy missed his calling. He should have been a poet.

THANKS

To the generous girls of the Scottish Rite D,
From a grateful but out-of-date old Ph.D.,
For whom they once made a most splendified cake,
By themselves did they mix, by themselves did they bake!

Lightened with soda and lighted with candles,
They brought it over to the senior of the Yandells,
To cheer him up on his nth birthday,
He being as old as Mathusaley.

In all the years of his scholastic life,
Into such a fine cake he ne'er had stuck knife,
'Twas iced on the edges and also on top,
Where also was growing a red candle crop.

Not to praise this great cake would be stupidly dumb,
'Twas soon eaten up to the very last crumb,
It was in sure truth, so delightfully nice,
Not even one crumb was left for the mice.

So thanks, many thanks, by way of "Sardine,"
For the loveliest cake that e'er I have seen.

—H. Y. BENEDICT*
The Sardine, Volume 7, 1929

The University of Texas' president's house was at one point just to the east of the dorm.

*Harry Yandell Benedict became a professor of applied mathematics and astronomy in 1907 and the tenth president of the University of Texas from 1927 until his sudden death from a cerebral hemorrhage May 10, 1937.

A Loving Witness

My daughter Mary Kathryn and her roommate were "potluck" roomies at SRD who could not have been more different. Mary Kathryn was an art history and Italian major and member of the Young Democrats. Michelle was a Plan 2,

McCombs Business School major, and the treasurer for the Young Republicans. Their room was divided in half with pro-choice and pro-life stickers, Bush vs. Kerry, etc, etc. You get the picture. Neither girl knew anyone else when they moved into the dorm and many of the girls on their floor were rooming with high school classmates so they both felt very alone and assumed the worst about each other.

In the midst of the Fall semester, Michelle's father died very suddenly of a heart attack. While most of the girls were sympathetic, they were scared to death, not knowing what to do or say. It was during that traumatic time that I became so impressed with the staff at SRD. They not only did the obvious caring things, they went the extra mile for Michelle and Mary Kathryn time and again.

I was so touched because, of course, they cared for Michelle, but they also understood how hard and frightening this was for Mary Kathryn to be with a roommate that, up until then was not her friend, and who was very emotional, needing major support. It was obvious that so many of the staff were responding from a deep faith perspective and they expressed that openly without being oppressive about it.

As a parent, it made a strong and lasting impression on me. Even though we were in Austin, I knew that I would have had the same sense of security about the care given Mary Kathryn even clear across the country. Mary Kathryn and Michelle became very close during that sad time and both recently graduated, each still cherishing the friendship.

—ROGER PAYNTER, SRD Father
Pastor, First Baptist Church, Austin

Recollections of Scottish Rite Dormitory

I entered The University of Texas in the Fall of 1952. My friend Fred Hansen from El Paso had told me about the A Bar Hotel, which was air-conditioned and near the campus, so I stayed there. Scottish Rite Dormitory was in view of my dorm, but I didn't really know what it was for awhile, only that a lot of pretty, nicely dressed girls were coming and going from the place, and that it was a stately building unlike most buildings where I came from.

For several years, that was it. The dorm and the girls were there, but as an aero-engineering student, I didn't have much time to socialize, and SRD and I just coexisted for three years.

In the Fall of my fourth year, I had a new roommate, Randy Duckworth from Dallas, who had a good friend, Virginia Hurley, with whom he had graduated from Woodrow Wilson High School, and who had opted to stay in SRD. Her dad, Randy Hurley, a Dallas builder, was a Mason, so SRD was the logical place for his daughter.

Randy arranged a double blind date for me with Virginia, which took me into SRD for the first time. I was impressed with the grandeur of it all, and with the tight security. But I scared her off with my aggressive driving, and that was that.

Until my fifth (senior) year. Randy again arranged a date for me with Virginia (who had decided that "Ginny" was a better appellation by this time), and we went to a formal Air Force ball. This time there was a real connection, and a few months later, I gave her an engagement ring while parked in my '53 Studebaker across from SRD, near All Saints' Church.

From then on, I was a regular there, eating with Ginny on Sundays in the dining room, where the food was excellent, and served by tidy waiters, one of whom, Tom Moser, also became my lifelong friend. Tom was dating Nelwyn Delaney, who was Ginny's roommate, so we went on a lot of double dates together, probably because I had a car that could get us from SRD to Mount Bonnell and the Lake Austin night spots.

I was commissioned into the Air Force on June 1, 1957, and married Virginia Lee Hurley in Dallas on June 8, exactly 50 years ago. We had three beautiful girls, Dawn, Ginger, and Sally, all of whom attended UT, and stayed at SRD. So I had many occasions to return to the dorm after a 20-year absence. What a different place it was! The place looked basically the same, but it was air-conditioned! And there was no security to speak of. Our girls could come and go at any hour of the day or night. I was disappointed about that.

My girls all went on to get degrees, two from UT, and are happy, productive citizens. Dawn works for Boeing on the Space Station program. Ginger is a special education teacher at Pillow Elementary School in Austin, and Sally is working in a law firm in San Antonio.

Ginny and I were very happily married until she died of a reaction to a prescription drug in July of 2002.

I live in Austin now, and frequently detour to drive by SRD. There are a lot of wonderful memories there.

—HUMBOLDT C. MANDELL, JR., PH.D.
SRD Husband and Father

Panty Raid!

Being "halfway between heaven and hell," located between the Fiji house and the seminary, we were always subject to panty raids from the frat pledges next door. One year during such a raid one girl opened a downstairs door to let in some boys. Other girls would throw underwear out the windows.

In my sister's time (1971-73) the dorm still was doing the girl's laundry so Mrs.Townes really got them when she reminded the girls after a panty raid that their names were on all their underwear!

It caused a bit of a ruffle in one panty raid during my tenure (1975-1979) when a *Daily Texan* photographer took a picture of a row of SRD girls looking out a window at the Fiji's serenading us in diapers. On the windowsill was a novelty radio shaped like a beer can so in the picture it appeared as if the SRD girls were drinking beer. Scandalous!

—CANDY ANDREWS
1975-1979

Mystery Man Gaily Strolls in SRD, Gladly Stampedes Out

At approximately 10:45 o'clock Monday night an unidentified young man was seen walking down the hall of the second floor of SRD. When he met a young co-ed on her way to the shower, he nonchalantly asked, "Where is room 247?"

The girl stared at him for a few minutes, then turned and led him straight to the room, announcing to the occupants, "You have a male visitor!"

A pajama-clad girl opened the door, quickly recovered herself, and tactfully asked, "Won't you come in, Jim?"

"Oh, no thank you, Jean," he answered. "I just thought I'd return your book to you since I have finished it. Thanks, and good night."

Jim started back down the hall, this time with all eyes on this brave character who dared to walk into a girl's dormitory.

Up to this point Jim had been acting right "at home," but on the way out he ran into one of the Scottish Rite matrons. At this meeting, he broke into a fast run that ended only when he was well on his way out the front walk.

SRD occupants didn't catch the boy to ask him whether he purposely entered no man's land in order to get his name in the headlines of the *Texan*, or whether he just made a slight mistake about the rules and regulations.

Matrons at the door of the dormitory later reported that a young man came in about this time and asked if he might take a book back to the girl's room. The matron said she told him yes, thinking he certainly knew that he must call for the young lady at the desk.

"Jim" remains unidentified.

—Rae Wright
The Daily Texan, circa 1944,
reprinted with permission

A Palace Full of Princesses

Scottish Rite Dorm, to a naive young freshman boy from North Texas, looked more like a castle than a women's residence hall. All of the ladies who lived there were princesses of charm and beauty. The few girls who I had met through my involvement with a campus religious organization did little to dispel my illusion. They displayed the appropriate royal charm that I anticipated. So when the opportunities came to date some from that palace I welcomed them with great enthusiasm.

The first lady I recall taking out who lived at SRD appeared to me as the most beautiful girl I had ever met. (Remember the bias of this young freshman to all residents of this hall.) She was of mixed ancestry from the Middle East and Asia; I was totally intimidated. I recall very few details of the evening—it was probably dinner and a movie—except that I borrowed my roommate's Mustang to impress her.

The car was much more impressive than my driving: while stopped at a traffic light I kept glancing over at her while she was staring out the window and sat through a couple of cycles of green. On at least the third cycle she finally turned to me and said, "Would you like to go this time or do you plan to sit here all night?" I think that may have been our last date but we remained friends.

I gained many friends who lived at SRD, so I became a frequent visitor in my sophomore year. In fact, it was difficult to determine, and keep track of, which girls were friends and which ones I hoped to be more than just friends.

This led to a very embarrassing situation when I was in the lobby to see one girl and another girl who I had been on a date with the previous week, and who I had not yet kept my promise to call soon, came down the stairs. I tap-danced around the awkwardness quick enough to assure her departure before the intended date appeared. I do not think I ever did call that first girl back.

One friend, who became more than just a friend, moved into the SRD palace shortly after our romance blossomed. This gave me the opportunity to attend the spring formal (cotillion?). This event appeared to me as the high point of the school year arranged to encourage romance for each princess and her date. However I recall arriving late, leaving early, and the dining room was appropriately dark but crowded. Neither of us were in the mood for romance as we soon after parted ways.

Scottish Rite Dorm holds some great memories although my time there was brief. After my sophomore year, I never visited the palace again. I never found my true love amongst all those fleeting yet passionate interests, awkward moments, and charming ladies. However I am sure they helped prepare me for my true princess who later captured my heart.

—DOUG KEENAN
SRD Suitor and
Visitor in No Man's Land

After Four Years

Up on Twenty-seventh Street, there is the best looking home with the prettiest lawn, the greenest shrubs, the shadiest trees, the grandest columns of colonial grandeur, the softest sofas, in fact, just a thoroughly "superlative" home called Scottish Rite Dormitory.

But that's not half of it—it's who lives there that we are "most glad" we know! No wonder we all succumb to the magic lure of those jovial and friendly inhabitants. (Even the boys here at my nominal abode, just three doors east, when they answer the phone call our place "Scottish Rite Annex.") I claim that a freshman couldn't have a pure heart if he had neglected making the acquaintanceship of SRD the first term of his first year.

A few days ago, Mrs. Slayter was meeting my family in the parlor. She remarked to my mother and father as she shook hands with Miriam, my older sister, "I never have known this one like the others (Laurie and myself) because she hasn't stayed up here with us like the other two have!"

Funny as it is, it was literally true. It isn't hard to give a reason. Just the same reason of hundreds of University boys. We feel like a week has been unsuccessful if we have not been over to Scottish Rite several times.

The last four years that I have gone past it dozens of times a day and gone in it nearly as many, it has become a real part of me—I love that eupeptic place and everything connected with it.

—HARPER BROWN
The Sardine, 1927

Parents' Memories of SRD

Sending a daughter off to college was a little frightening, but having her live at SRD certainly did alleviate some of those fears! Laura King moved into SRD in the Fall of 1997, her first year of college. Living in that wonderful historic house (in spite of the mildew and wild elevator rides) was special and certainly added to the excitement of college life. It was fun to help decorate the corner room with the huge windows looking out over the grounds and the old live oak trees. We loved visiting on Parents Weekend, and shared in the joy of graduation celebrations, birthday parties, and a wedding shower in the Rec Room.

Actually, there is history at SRD for us as parents even before our daughter arrived. Her brother, Matthew King, was on the wait staff in the cafeteria for several years and our future daughter-in-law, Amie Stone, was a resident at the time. Matthew had his pick of all the lovely young residents but chose the "cream of the crop" as he served her soup and CCB's!

—DON AND JOANNE KING
SRD Parents

Pizza and a Cadillac

In 1964 I dated a girl from SRD. Her daddy was a 32nd degree Mason, which meant he was very high on the food chain. I quickly found out about all of the dorm's rules but never actually entered the building. For our dates we met off the premises, spending a lot of time at the Rome Inn, a pizza place on 29th Street, which is where Texas French Bread is now located. The same location later became a nightspot where Stevie Ray Vaughn played.

We also frequented the Americana Theater for movies, but one of my favorite things about our dates was driving her father's 1956 Cadillac. It was so much fun to drive, and I was super careful. I remember being duly impressed by the stately manner of the SRD and figured if I was going to be

allowed to hang around, I would need to stay on the straight
and narrow.

—JOHN WHEAT
SRD Suitor, Archives Translator
Center for American History

The SRD—An Outsider's Opinion

To the outsider—and my views must by nature be those of
the male outsider—the Scottish Rite Dormitory is a palace of
luxurious comfort, of intriguing mystery, of irritating inconvenience.

The young man who pays his first respects to a resident of
the Scottish Rite Dormitory must needs approach that auspi-
cious structure with a feeling of mingled fear and wonder-
ment. He looks upon a stately building. There is a carefully
kept lawn. There are trees, and flowers, and walks, and
benches. What is behind the castle and the courtyard, or how
far back it extends, he can consider only in speculation. If it is
night, he beholds the entire majestic scene in the dazzling bril-
liance of innumerable electric lamps which fill the premises
with an atmosphere of carnival.

Under such circumstances, the bravest of men—even ath-
letes—are unable to present a full show of calmness and equa-
nimity as they walk up to the threshold, knowing that behind
the portals which they are about to enter are domiciled over
three hundred women—all college girls! And never should it
be forgotten that they are Masons' daughters.

A complete recovery from this initial fear and uneasiness
is rarely effected until after more than six or seven timorous
entrances have been made. Such primary embarrassment having been dispelled, however, there are many visitors who begin
to take advantage of a good thing; there are certain gentlemen,
such as they may be, who spend so much time within the
dorm or its environs that they would surely be mistaken for inmates were it not fairly well known that housing accommoda-
tions are offered only to the fairer and more deadly of the
species.

These liberal visits are inspired by three things for which

the dorm is universally renowned: first, the comfortable advantages which the dormitory allows; second, the graciousness of the matrons; and third, the compelling and alluring personalities of the various residents who are the objects of these enduring dates.

For although it is remarkably well understood that all Scottish Rite girls do not stagger under the weight of medals won at beauty contests, it is quite as remarkably well understood that they are tremendously interesting and alluring.

—DAVID MILLER
The Annual Sardine, May 1926

A Memorable History

Masons Take First Steps
to House Daughters
at University of Texas

Main Building of Lubbock Hall Dormitory Leased For Two Years By Texas Scottish Rite Masons, Austin secretary; Mike H. Thomas and W. C. Temple of Dallas, D. W. McLeod and T. J. Holbrook of Galveston, D. R. Woodward Jr. of Austin, J. J. Ormsbee and Crawford Harvie of El Paso and J. K. Blackstone of San Antonio.

Lubbock Hall—the old Presbyterian Theological Seminary property—is within three blocks of the university campus. The main building consists of a three-story fireproof, steam-heated, brick dormitory.

There are also four brick residences, two of which are immediately available for dormitory purposes, and a large brick dining room with capacity to seat 1,000 students. This dormitory with 70 girls, is under charge of Mrs. J. Ed Kauffman as director and Mrs. Martha R. Johnson as business manager.

Driskill Hall, on Whitis Avenue, a large dwelling house with a rooming capacity of 30, was also leased by the Masons and is now occupied by daughters of Texas Masons. These girls, who are under the charge of Mrs. Walter Acker, take their meals at the Lubbock Hall dining room.

These buildings have been leased for two years. Their use is only temporary, according to Judge McClendon. In the meantime adequate grounds will be purchased and the construction of a girls' dormitory and other buildings which may prove advisable, states Judge McClendon.

Judge Cochran calls attention to the students' revolving fund, which is being organized by the Scottish Rite Masons of Texas for the purpose of assisting students who need financial aid. The cost of assisting one person for a year is estimated at $300 for dormitory accommodations alone and $500 for all expenses. Already several individual Masons and some Masonic bodies have offered to provide for the expense of one student each.

—*SAN ANTONIO EXPRESS*
October 31, 1920

Architecture Is Important

Herbert M. Greene, Dallas architect, was born in Huntington, Pennsylvania, in 1871. In 1876 the family moved to Peoria, Illinois, where he received his early schooling. He subsequently attended the University of Illinois and graduated with a Bachelor of Science degree in architecture in 1893. He practiced architecture briefly in Peoria before moving to Dallas in 1897. There he operated his own office until 1900, when he formed a partnership with James P. Hubbell under the name Hubbell and Greene. During the first two decades of the twentieth century Greene produced a large number of important works, including the Dallas News Building, the Scottish Rite Dormitory for Girls in Austin, the Dallas Trust and Savings Bank, Westminster and Oak Cliff Presbyterian churches in Dallas, Temple Emanu-El in Dallas, the Neiman-Marcus Building in Dallas, and Scottish Rite cathedrals in Dallas, El Paso, San Antonio, and Joplin, Missouri.

—HANDBOOK OF TEXAS ONLINE

What's in a Name?

Mr. Charles Wesley Whitis was born in 1824 near Rogersville, Hawkins County, Tennessee. He married Florence Rogan in 1857. Their children included Mary, Rufus, Willie B., John H., Charles Wesley Jr., Florence, Ellen Patten, Gertrude, and Thomas P.

Whitis received his B.A. degree about 1852 from Tusculum College in Greenville, North Carolina, and was a clerk of the District Court in Greenville. In December 1854 he moved to Lockhart, Texas, where he became a leading figure in the community.

After the Civil War, he bought 60 acres of land in North Austin and lived with his family in a cottage at what is now the corner of Alice and 38th streets.

Whitis formed a partnership with James H. Raymond and bought the private banking firm of Swenson Brothers, and in 1871 helped bring the first railroad, The Houston and Texas

Central, to Austin. The City Council of Austin changed Berlin and Matilde streets to Whitis Avenue* after his death.

Connection to UT: At one time Mr. Whitis owned most of the land on which UT is currently situated. Grace Hall, All Saints Chapel, and Gregg House are located where the Whitis' orchard once stood. The "new" house for his family was built on the site where the Austin Scottish Rite Dormitory now stands.

*Whitis Avenue borders SRD on the west side.

Dedication Services of New Scottish Rite Dormitory Are Held Thanksgiving Morning

Releasing two snow-white doves, emblematic of peace, purity, and love, Samuel P. Cochran of Dallas, sovereign grand inspector general of the Scottish Rite of Freemasonry of the Southern Jurisdiction of the United States, dedicated the new Scottish Rite Dormitory to God and to the service of humanity, for the education of the young women of Texas.

Cochran Dedicates Dormitory

Fully a thousand people were present at the dedication ceremonies which took place on Thanksgiving morning at 10 o'clock in front of the dormitory, stressing in his brief address the fact that the present time is a day of enlightenment and that we are coming more and more to the realization that woman is a really important factor in the intellectual life of the world, and that it is necessary that the training given in the young women of today be as intensive and thorough as that given to the young men. As Mr. Cochran released the doves, he said a prayer on behalf of the young womanhood of the University of Texas now occupying the dormitory. The doves circled several times in the air and finally came to rest upon the dome of the main dormitory.

Johnson and Neff Speak

D. Frank Johnson of Waco, Grand Master of the Masonic

Lodge in Texas, followed Mr. Cochran, speaking on "Masonry." He outlined briefly the main Masonic doctrines, emphasizing the fact that the Masons are pledged to keep the principles of education and enlightenment.

Governor Neff, who was the next speaker, spoke on the relation of character building to education. He praised the educational work of Texas Masons, saying that the good works of this noble order shall live forever.

Vinson Praises Work

President Robert E. Vinson, speaking on "The University," reviewed the past few years of the University's progress and the trials through which it has passed. He expressed the hope that more of such magnificent buildings will be erected to help make the University one of the first class.

McClendon Presents Flag

Judge J. W. McClendon, of the Commission of Appeals, speaking on "The Dormitory," pointed to the dormitory as a material expression of the ideals of Freemasonry. In conclusion, he presented to the dormitory board an American flag from the home of George Washington and a box of growing ivy taken from Washington's tomb, the gifts of Mrs. T. S. Maxey.

The ceremonies finished, the visitors were officially introduced to the girls of the dormitory, and everyone who wished was shown the interior of the dormitory from top to bottom.

—MIKE J. KIPPENBROCK
The Daily Texan, December 2,
1922, reprinted with permission

New Scottish Rite Dormitory Dedicated by Texas Masons

CEREMONY IN CHARGE OF SAM P. COCHRAN
INCLUDES SEVERAL APPROPRIATE ADDRESSES

Formal dedication of the Scottish Rite Dormitory for women attending the University of Texas took place this morning at 10 o'clock when ceremonies appropriate for the occasion were held at the dormitory on Twenty-seventh street near Whitis and University avenues.

The dedication was in charge of Hon. Sam P. Cochran, 33rd degree, Sovereign Grand Inspector General of Masonic bodies in Texas, who delivered the opening address. It was Mr. Cochran who first conceived the idea of the erection of the dormitory to house daughters of Masons while attending the University.

Other addresses were made as follows: "Masonry" by Frank Johnson, 32, grandmaster of Masons in Texas. "The State" by Hon. Pat M. Neff, governor of Texas; "The University" by Dr. Robert E. Vinson, president of the University of Texas; "The Dormitory" by Hon. James W. McClendon, 33.

Following the addresses the following persons were introduced: Sam P. Cochran, Dallas; W. C. Temple, Dallas; F. H. Sparrow, Ft. Worth; D. W. McLeod, Galveston; T. J. Holbrook, Galveston; J. J. Ormsbee, El Paso; Crawford Harvie, El Paso; Jas. W. McClendon, Austin; W. S. Fly, San Antonio; and John K. Blackstone, San Antonio, all directors of the Scottish Rite Educational Association of Texas; and the following members of the dormitory staff: Mrs. J. Ed Kauffman, director; Mrs. J. S. Myrick, Mrs. John G. Slayter, and Mrs. S. H. Lawhon, assistant directors; Mrs. Martha R. Johnson, business manager; Miss Selma Streit, dietician.

—*AUSTIN AMERICAN-STATESMAN*
©1922, reprinted with permission

Arm Bands

The girls from Scottish Rite wear bands
Inscribed with SRD
And people at these letters wonder—
What can their meaning be?
Now we know what it's all about
But we'll just let it ride
It means they're Stately and Refined
And also Dignified.

—*THE ANNUAL SARDINE*
Volume 1, #1, 1922–1923

How Do You Like Staying in a Modern Dormitory?

From the first Thanksgiving in 1922 until the fall of 1937 there were no individual phones. Only two lines coming in and out were had for the entire dormitory in 1922, and ten in 1937. Buzzers were used in the rooms.

First floor in 1937 had two phones, second had five, third had five, and fourth had none. Complaints were rife. Twelve phones with only ten lines in and out, counting the long distance lines, for over three hundred girls were not enough. Another objection to this system was that when a girl rushed to a phone to answer her buzz, the phones were generally already in use. Then would come the mad dash up and down stairs—from one phone to another, from one floor to another, in an attempt to find a free phone. Quite frequently by that time the person calling grew tired and hung up. If the girl did get to talk, always was there an interested audience of at least five waiting to grab the phone the minute she put it down.

So the girls coming to the dormitory in the fall of 1937 found a phone in every room. Now a girl can tell her true love that he is her one and only in privacy—if the transom is up and she doesn't talk too loudly. Or, again she may scream at him if she chooses. No one but her roommate is around listening.

Another advantage is that it is much simpler to call in and out of the dormitory now since two lines have been added.

Another improvement that perhaps many of the girls are not so aware of is the new building in back of SRD housing the laundry and boiler room, which were formerly located in the basement of the main building.

Built of red tapestry brick to match the main building, this new construction cost approximately $42,800. It consists of a laundry room, the power plant, two dressing rooms, and nine garages. The garages serve as godsends to those Sardinites who owning cars formerly left them outside all night or had them stored away from the dormitory.

SRD keeps up with the world, you see. And this year it has again taken the lead in modernization!

—*The Sardine*, 1938

Dear Santa Claus

December 23, 1923

We venture to write you just a word
To let you know in season,
As Christmas time draws near
What Mother Kauffman's children
Would like to have this year.

Natalie needs a six-foot bed;
Her own is much too small
Perhaps that is the reason
She never grows at all.

And bring a mild bandanna
For Sybil's woolly head,
For way down South in Dixie
Where she was born and bred.

Agatha says her bonnet
Is sadly out of date.
(She hasn't had a new one
Since 1898!)

We'd like a set of dishes—
Our old one's nearly gone,
For half the pitchers are broken,
And half the glasses are pawned.

The spoons have long been missing,
And all of us agree
That forks are not convenient
When one is sipping tea.

Please bring a little carriage
Kathryn Lemly begs,
She suffers from dyspepsia
Because of weakly legs.

As walking's not much pleasure
She rarely ventures out

And feels she'd soon be better
If she could drive about.
                    —*The Annual Sardine*
                    Volume 2, #1, 1923

Gifts to the Dormitory

A radio—Mr. Lem Scarbrough
A flag which flew on Mount Vernon—Mrs. T. S. Maxey
Grandfather clock—Mr. Albert Linz
The flagpole—Girls of 1923-24
A piece of tapestry—Mr. E. M. Scarbrough
The beginning of our library—Bartholemew class
Books for the library—*Sardine* staff of 1925
A Texas flag—*Sardine* staff of 1925
A silver vase—Seniors of 1925
Brass candlesticks—Girls of the dormitory at Christmas, 1925
Donation toward andirons—Mr. Blanderman
"Fritzie," a registered German roller canary—Hyde Park Floral
    Co.
The loan of *Alabama Peach Orchard* by the Austin Art League
                    —*The Sardine*
                    May 1926

Scottish Rite Girls Celebrate Raising of Flag from Mt. Vernon

Austin Scouts Plant Ivy Clipped From Mt. Vernon Home;
Donated by Mrs. Maxey.

Ceremonial services were scheduled to take place this afternoon at 3:30 o'clock at the Scottish Rite dormitory in honor of the raising of a flag there which once floated over Mt. Vernon, home of George Washington, and which was presented to the dormitory last year by Mrs. T. S. Maxey, regent for many years at the Mt. Vernon home.

A staff flag has been made and presented by the girls of the hall to be used in flying the flag permanently over the dormitory. An official flag raiser will be on hand to raise and lower the flag each day from now on at the dormitory.

The Boy Scouts of Austin, who are the possessors of a large ivy plant clipped from an ivy growth at the Mt. Vernon home and donated to that organization by Mrs. Maxey, have agreed to plant the growth at the dormitory since the flag will be there, and both of these objects of prized value come from the Washington home. They were invited to take part in the ceremony this afternoon, and a delegation of the members were on hand to plant the ivy. A group of the local Girl Scouts were also present at the ceremony on an invitation from the dormitory.

Judge Fly of San Antonio accepted an invitation to make a talk at the ceremony and talked on subject appropriate to the occasion, bringing in the life of the Father of Our Country and giving the significance that the flag and ivy had about it, coming from the old home of Washington.

A colonial tea was scheduled to be held in the social room of the dormitory following the ceremony, and a colonial play arranged by the girls of the dormitory was to be held in the auditorium after the tea.

—THE DAILY TEXAN, 1923
reprinted with permission

Dorm Receives Colonial Clock

A Grandfathers clock, given as a gift from Albert Linz of Linz Bros. Jewelry* in Dallas, was installed at the Scottish Rite Dormitory Wednesday morning by Carl Mayer Jewelry of this city, according to Mrs. Ed Kauffman, director of the dormitory.

One day in September, Linz and Judge McClendon met together at a social affair in Boston, and Linz remarked that he had never seen the dormitory, but he wished to give some gift. This clock came at Judge McClendon's suggestion. It has been placed on the east side of the social room of the dormitory.

—THE DAILY TEXAN, 1923
reprinted with permission

*Linz Brothers "Jewelists" (copyrighted name) opened for business in

Dallas in 1899 and supplied anything from diamond encrusted dog barrettes to oil derrick stickpins for the newly rich. Brother Albert was known for giving customers horehound candy for defense against colds.

Scottish Rite Girls to Formulate System of Self Government

According to Mrs. J. Ed. Kaufman, director, plans are being formulated by the young women of the Scottish Rite Dormitory, for the organization of a system of self-government. It is expected that the plans will be accomplished and in full force before the beginning of the spring term.

"The matter of self-government will be in the hands of the young women," said Mrs. Kaufman. "Officers will be selected from the upper classmen, whose duty it will be to form rules and regulations, and direct the government of student life in the dormitory. Committees will be appointed in charge of the study hours and social and house affairs."

Mrs. Kaufman is heartily in accord with the idea of the self-government system. In her opinion, it will have the effect of making the girls more interested in the dormitory and in preserving their high standard of conduct.

—THE DAILY TEXAN
January 25, 1923
reprinted with permission

Scottish Rite Dormitory

It would be difficult to find anywhere a more interesting portrayal of true character than is found in the Scottish Rite Dormitory for daughters of Master Masons at the University of Texas. The process through which such an end was reached and the extent of its success is one of widespread interest to all Masons.

Early in the year 1920, Sam P. Cochran, Sovereign Grand Inspector General in Texas, submitted the proposition for the erection of the Scottish Rite Dormitory to the various Bodies of the Rite in this state, and appealed to them for their support and cooperation. Primarily the purpose of this was to provide suitable living quarters for the daughters of Master Masons attending the University, and to surround them with a wholesome environment. A secondary object was to aid the University in its housing problem. The response from the various bodies was unanimous and in order to put the movement into immediate operation, Mr. Cochran secured a lease for two years upon the Presbyterian Theological Seminary property beginning September 1, 1920.

In the latter part of September 1920, the project began with Lubbock Hall, 100 East 27th Street, accommodating 50 girls under the directorship of Mrs. J. Ed Kauffman; Annex A, 100 East 27th Street, accommodating 11 girls under the directorship of Mrs. Martha R. Johnson; Driskill Hall, 2610 Whitis Avenue, accommodating 30 girls under the directorship of Mrs. Walter Acker of Commerce, Texas; Annex B, 104 East 27th Street, accommodating 11 girls under the directorship of Mrs. Lena Jones. It is interesting to note that Miss Katrina Kirby of Dallas was the first girl to file application in 1920.

With an upper hold on affairs thus far, the Scottish Rite Educational Association of Texas, which consisted of Sam P. Cochran, Dallas, Texas, as president; James W. McClendon, Austin, as vice president; W. S. Fly, San Antonio, as second vice president; Joe H. Muenster, Austin, as secretary; and H. A. Wroe, Austin, as treasurer, began the erection of a dormitory which was to accommodate 306 girls, having a total of 169 rooms.

The Georgian style was chosen as the basis of design for the exterior, and a dormitory erected which is one of the most beautiful structures in Texas and which is looked upon with admiration and respect by all those who are fortunate enough to know of its splendid work. The funds for the erection of the dormitory were obtained by pledging of the bodies to give for its support one-half of the gross revenue derived from initiation fees for the three years, beginning with 1920, and one-third of such revenues for the following two years.

September 1922 found the dormitory ready for use, and

operations began with Mrs. J. Ed. Kauffman as director; Mrs. Martha R. Johnson as business manager; Miss Selma Streit as dietitian; and Mrs. J. S. Myrick, Mrs. John G. Slayter, and Mrs. S. K. Lawhorn as assistant directors. This arrangement has continued to the present time with the exception of Miss Selma Streit being made business manager, and Miss George LaRue, dormitory nurse.

The number of girls in the dormitory has grown from the 102 who filed applications in 1922 to its full capacity of the present time.

No history of the Scottish Rite Dormitory would be complete without a mention at least of its traditions. With the primary object in mind as stated by Mr. Cochran in his proposal for the construction of the dormitory, those in charge set about to create a home-like atmosphere and to make the girls as comfortable and as happy as possible. The various traditions which grew out of this purpose include February 22, Washington's Birthday Tea; Thanksgiving dinner, and the formal Christmas dinner. Along with these are Senior teas, special dinners for the Masons, and formal dances.

The dormitory was dedicated November 30, 1922, by the late Brother D. Frank Johnson of Brownwood, Grand Master of Masons in Texas at that time. At the dedication Gov. Pat Neff delivered an address on "The State." Other addresses were delivered by Dr. Robert E. Vinson, at the time president of the University of Texas, and Judge James W. McClendon, now Past Grand Master.

The records show that 121 Scottish Rite Dormitory girls have graduated with honors during this period from June 1923 to June 1935. During this period the total number of dormitory girls who have graduated from the University of Texas is approximately 951.

Directors of the Scottish Rite Educational Association having in charge the affairs of the dormitory are: Sam P. Cochran, President, Dallas; Jas. W. McClendon, Vice President, Austin; P. D. Mathis, Second Vice President, San Antonio; D. K. Woodward, Third Vice President, Austin; H. A. Wroe, Treasurer, Austin; Directors: Walter C. Temple, Dallas; T. J. Holbrook, Galveston; D. W. McLeod, Galveston; Jewel P. Lightfoot, Fort Worth; Scott C. White, El Paso; Dr. F. P. Miller,

El Paso; Dr. A. C. McDaniel, San Antonio; W. C. Ragan, Houston; Geo. E. Kepple, Houston; D. K. Woodward, Austin; P. D. Mathis, San Antonio.

—*TEXAS GRAND LODGE* MAGAZINE
August 1935

SRD Seniors Honored at Tea

SRD Seniors were complimented with a garden party Thursday from 5:30 to 7:30 o'clock. The SRD staff was in charge of the party, which has become a dormitory tradition.

On the lawn back of the dormitory, seniors greeted their classmates, board of directors of SRD, professors, and friends.

The maypole dance which has grown to be another of the dormitory's traditions, was given twice during the evening in order that all guests might see it.

—*THE DAILY TEXAN*
reprinted with permission

The Matrons

They are people who inhabit the realm above us, and tell us we can or can't go out at ten o'clock in the night to buy a hamburger, and sympathize when we have the toothache and smile at the things we say, and sometimes, don't smile. They supply necessary articles like provender [food], and that type of gentle, insistent authority that youth demands, and they believe in us through it all, and hope desperately for the best.

Mrs. Kauffman sits at her desk in the room with one long window and impresses us with the duties of our position, even as she instills within us respect and affection for the home we live in. Infinitely she is fitted for her directorship for she has seen the vision of the magnitude of our institution's foundation. Thus she encourages high idealism and loftier principles day by day as she smiles above the collection of meal receipts and sign-out tablets.

Miss Streit is a lady who is dear to the heart every hour but particularly three times a day. She is one of those capable persons who is so efficient that you never notice it, which is indeed the quintessence of capability. She has a faculty for entertaining three hundred businessmen or Ted Shawn with the noiselessness of most ordinary occasions. She searches for Epicurean delights with which to relieve the monotony of mastication, and renders mere food a poem.

They say Mrs. Myrick keeps peace on second floor and her own disposition at the same time. Her personality is the sort that lends itself, and she speaks with an aristocratic little twist of the tongue that reminds one of crinoline and the old South—and then, Duchess belongs to her.

Mrs. Slayter wears silver gray linen dresses to match her hair, but her eyes are gay, and her laugh could belong to no one but a girl. The third floor corridor capitulates before her irresistible charm, and even enjoys being scolded about making their beds.

Mrs. Lawhon is at home in a room on fourth floor, and there are always fresh flowers there, and thrilly little bird notes. Mrs. Lawhon is one of those rare superiors who hasn't forgotten how to be a good sport, and that is the strongest sort of bid for fame.

Sometimes when we feel the sagging weight of our textbook on the homeward way, somebody rattles up alongside and asks us to ride. That's Mrs. Johnson. She is the lady who always seems to have a clinging aura of board bills, and makes subtle remarks about the expense of electricity, but always grins, and has other urgent affairs when she happens in and discovers us surreptitiously removing bananas and other booty from the table from our mail box where we have stowed them.

They know a lot, the Superiors. They are cognizant of the young man's name who calls around on Saturday night, and every time we flunk a course some hidden power informs them. They even know when the Satanic influence tempts us to depart for class leaving the bed unmade, and still they smile and hope desperately for the best.

—THE ANNUAL SARDINE
Volume 2, #1, 1923

Sardine Dedicated to Mrs. Kauffman

Yes, the *Sardine* came out again this year, its sixteenth, just as planned, before the Scottish Rite Dormitory girls left school for summer vacation. Responsible for it are Constance Matula, editor, and Mary Katherine Settegast, business manager.

Other members of the staff are Mary Helen Hall, assistant business manager; Margaret Gidley, art editor; and Martha Woodson and Fannie Machles, reporters.

The issue is dedicated to Mrs. J. Ed Kauffman, who is leaving SRD this year. She has been director since its opening in 1922. In the dedication the editor writes, "It is truly her dormitory, her girls, her book."

Besides pictures of the directors of the dormitory and the house council, the seniors are grouped in one section with the underclassmen in another. By each name of a senior is a one-word adjective which describes her.

The pages of the book to which the girls most look forward prior to its distribution are the pictures of the six favorites, selected by vote of the residents and unknown until the book appears.

They are Mary Casey of Houston, Kappa Kappa Gamma; Hazel Ross Deputy, Delta, Delta, Delta from Brownsville; Janette Hicks, Zeta Tau Alpha from Fort Worth; Matilda Real, Chi Omega from Keerbille [sic]; Constance Matula of Runge, Alpha Delta Pi; and Margaret Weinert, Brownville, Zeta Tau Alpha.

The book contains members of honor societies living in SRD and those who made the honor roll the fall semester. Also there is gossip and notes on the characteristics of different girls. One of the best features is the snapshot sections showing dormitory life.

> —THE SUMMER TEXAN
> June 7, 1938
> reprinted with permission

A Tale of Two Bevos

Four years after Bevo II was sent ingloriously back to pasture, perhaps the unlikeliest Bevo of them all appeared on the scene. History has done its best to forget the first Bevo III. He is no longer reckoned in the line of succession and appears in precious few sources. Both his origin and his fate are unknown.

Why the historical blackballing? Perhaps it's because this longhorn mascot had a shameful secret: he wasn't a longhorn at all. He was a Hereford steer.

Despite that impediment, this Bevo (let's call him IIIa) remained in office for two years. His activity, however, seems to have been limited to leading two parades from Scottish Rite Dormitory to the Library Building. There is no record of him ever entering the stadium. Maybe the Athletic Council was still wary to give approval, given the problems with the first two Bevos.

—*ALCALDE*
reprinted with permission

SRD To Hear Game

Girls of the Scottish Rite Dormitory will follow the progress of the Texas-Harvard game at a radio dinner at 1 o'clock today. A wire has been leased and loud speakers have been set up in the dining room of the dormitory so that the girls will not miss the first part of the game during the noon hour.

—*THE DAILY TEXAN*, circa 1920s
reprinted with permission

Famous Sayings

"Punch my buzzer quick."
"Lend me your hat."
"Who has a cake of soap?"
"Let's go up the other side and get another sack."
"Is Bea's open yet?"
"Be sure and remember to come to chapel in the morning."
"What time is it somebody?"
"Does anybody have some ink?"

"Annie, have I had a call?"

"Leave the lights on just a minute!"

"Girls, please make up these beds on the east sleeping porch."

"Everyone have your rooms clean and your doors open."

"Who has my book?"

"Will you call me when you get through with the iron?"

"May I have this dance?"

—THE ANNUAL SARDINE

Volume 1, #1, 1922–1923

Annie

Would this book of SRD's be complete without a page for Annie? Why, of course not. Who would answer any of the following questions if it weren't for Annie? "Did I get any calls?" "Who called me downstairs?" "Will you tell him I'm not here?" "Have I a package?"

"Have you seen my book? I left it in the social room. I can't study without it." "What did the boy look like?" "Well, did he say he would come back?"

Annie's unfailing answers are always right. Her popularity with the girls was shown the night of the SRD Christmas tree. Annie got more presents and more cheers than anyone in the house.

She is so well liked that the girls fuss when she is not here after 8:30 o'clock on Saturday and not on Sunday. They miss her. She is always so obliging about taking a letter out to the box and is always willing to help the girls out of their difficulties.

Perhaps we do not know it, but Annie is a keen student of human nature or perhaps I should say "girl" nature. She studies the girls and recognizes them by sight, name, and voice a few days after school starts.

Annie likes to know that she can remember nearly all of the girls who have ever lived in the dormitory. She is very proud of the fact that she has been with the dormitory since within about three months of its opening.

She tells with glee about the man who was so certain that a girl lived in SRD that he refused to even accept Mrs.

Kauffman's word that she did not. Finally, when a student directory was produced and it was proved that the girl lived at Kirby Hall, Annie had the laugh on the man because she had said at the first that no such girl lived here. And she had suggested too that he try Kirby Hall!

Not only is Annie popular with the girls. A certain boy asked his date one night if she knew who he liked best at Scottish Rite. (The girl was from Sardee.) She bit like all girls will and said:

"No, who?"

Well the boy was serious, so the girl got left because he said, "I like Annie."

—*THE SARDINE*
Volume 7, 1929

Rahs and Rants

Things We've Enjoyed Most—
The bull sessions ... midnight parties ... suppers on the lawn ... mail ... meals ... packages from home ... Annie's chuckle ... clean laundry ... formal dinners ... SRD's famous standards ... flowers on the table.

Things That Hack Us Most—
Getting up in the morning ... chicken every Sunday ... stamp borrowers ... cigarette bummers ... waiting for an outside line ... coming in at 11 ... gathering up the laundry ... the day the sheets are changed.

—*THE SARDINE*, 1940

On Dormitory Life

One who has not associated with many girls will find life in a dormitory very interesting. The flattering compliment of "you are different" can challenge. Every girl is "different." There are some distinct types, however, in a dormitory and those who belong to the types are enthusiastic about their special lines.

The athletic girl is muscular, jolly, and friendly. She scorns all the attention from men, but sympathetically enjoys the confidences of other less strong-minded friends.

The literary type of girl tries the age-old method of showing her eccentricity by deviating from the present-day styles of dress. Her femininity asserts itself so that her mode of dress diverges from that of others slightly. If she has long hair and pretty ears, she brazenly exposes her ears. If she has bobbed hair void of curl, she plasters it down until it is quite sleek. Both styles are suited to the types of beauty of the non-conformists, and yet they satisfy the craving for individuality, and assert the claims of genius.

The flapper type of girl is the prodigious borrower. One could almost endure her ceaseless chatter of men, and "good-looking" cares if it were not for the fact that she feels it to be a sacred duty in impressing each new victim to combine the various wardrobes of her floor, borrowed, even in the absence of the owner by means of irresistible sweet little notes.

The mischievous girl is usually very young and frolicsome. She takes great delight in mussing rooms gloriously, especially on Saturday nights, so that the tired tenant can come home her allotted few minutes after twelve, limping in the new silver slippers that just could trip through the last dance, to find the contents of her closet in the middle of her bed, the lights out, and the candle lost. It is small wonder college girls are often driven to profanity.

The most tiresome girl in the dormitory is the philosophical, sweetly serious girl. She has good advice by the bulk, which she deals out impartially to all. Every experience that one can have recalls to her mind similar experiences of her own, which she glibly recites to all within range of her voice. Her philosophy is trite and she utters age-old truths with the pride of discovery.

Many movements sweep over the dormitory, but the principal one occurs just before the first of every month. Auction sales wax exciting—evening dresses are offered for sale at a mere pittance, but nobody can buy. Financiers spring up overnight, and the most amazing propensities for business are developed.

A fellow conspirator and I spied one of these business geniuses whose particular activity was giving dancing lessons. Many of whom we would never have suspected of having terpsichorean [dancing] aspirations were there, eager with anticipation. The teacher made her class engage in all kinds of childish antics such as jumping, hopping, skipping, and swinging arms about like windmills. After they were quite exhausted, she gave a lengthy and impressive lecture on the joys of dancing and her philanthropic motives for teaching dancing. In conclusion she casually said: "Now you all please bring your five dollars for this course of ten lessons—tomorrow night."

Dormitory life is wonderfully enlightening to one who is interested in her own character. If one isn't interested in her character at first, she can't remain indifferent very long. Truth parties are the popular means of giving vent to ill feelings conventionally under the guise of a missionary spirit of helpfulness. A few compliments are put in to ease the pain of the more scathing criticisms, but one must never become angry. It simply isn't done at a truth party and one is seldom guilty of such an indiscretion, though her very soul is torn to shreds and exposed before the public eye.

Dormitory life is an education. She who comes out unscathed, I am sure, can brave the unknown world. The merits and demerits of this life, I feel that I cannot adequately discuss—but it is full of experiences and joys and applications that cannot be obtained at any other college place of abode.

—THE ANNUAL SARDINE
Volume 1, #1, 1922-1923

UT Seal Motto Is Translation
of Mirabeau B. Lamar Statement

"Disciplina praesidium civitatis" is not the name of a fraternity or a new kind of cocktail, but the motto appearing on the seal of The University of Texas. The seal, that combination of a book, star, and shield, appears on notebook covers and library book plates.

The motto is a translation by Edwin W. Fay, former Latin professor, of Mirabeau B. Lamar's statement, "Education is the safeguard of democracy."

The seal of the University has not always been as it is now. The first seal, devised November 15, 1881, was quite different from the seal we know today. The original consisted of a star inscribed by a decorative design of leaves. The Latin words, *Universitas Texana*, and the motto, *Non sine pulvere palma*, were inscribed around the circle.

For some reason this seal was seldom used, the seal of the State of Texas being used instead on official papers and other documents. The seal was found, however, in the corner of diplomas.

On October 22, 1902, Dr. W. J. Battle proposed that the University should adopt a new official seal.

The seal proposed by Dr. Battle and drawn by Charles Young of Philadelphia was adopted three years later. The only change made in this design was the use of English rather than Latin words, except for the motto.

—*THE DAILY TEXAN*
September 3, 1943
reprinted with permission

UT Column

Believe it or not, the Main Library is named after one of the founders of Texas, Mirabeau B. Lamar.

A coed recently was running from library to library in an attempt to trace down the Lamar Library. She was referred to the Main Library. She approached a page there and inquired if he knew where the Lamar Library was. He went to Lorena Baker, main librarian, and asked her.

"My dear young man," Miss Baker said, "don't you know where you work?"

A notice was posted on the bulletin board informing all employees of the library where they are working.

—CHARLIE SMITH
The Daily Texan, April 27, 1962,
reprinted with permission

Mirabeau B. Lamar was the second president of the Republic of Texas. For many years SRD gave the "Mirabeau B. Lamar" award to a graduating senior who excelled scholastically and in the realm of service.

Coy SRDines Hang Mistletoe to Catch Cadets at Formal

Mid holly, mistletoe, and peppermint canes, Scottish Rite Dormitory will entertain Naval pre-flight cadets with a Christmas formal dance Saturday night at the dormitory with the San Marcos Air Field Orchestra, the "Navitones," playing for dancing.

Both the ballroom and the living room will be cleared for dancing, Marjorie Logan, upper class adviser chairman of the dormitory, announced. The sixteen-piece musical unit of the Four Hundred and Twenty-Sixth American Air Force will play for dancing from 8:30 until 12 o'clock.

It is SRD tradition that the girls bring children's toys to their annual Christmas party for distribution to Austin children. Billy Jane Chandler, social chairman, announced that the toys would be collected around the Christmas tree at midnight, while the cadets and SRDines sing Christmas carols.

Chaperones will include Miss Selma Streit, director, Mrs. A. P. Dohoney, social director; and Miss Mary Jane Davis, Miss Margie Muse, and Mrs. William Miles, associate social directors.

—The Daily Texan
December 14, 1943
reprinted with permission

News of D-Day Arrives on the Campus

A slow, early morning rain fell steadily. Low in the northeast lightning flashed cautiously of a creeping, storm-black cloud, as the treetops stirred restively in the first breezes of a chill rain-wind.

On the radio, network dance orchestras wavered, sputtered and crackled with storm static. At 2:30 o'clock [A.M.], sleepy-toned announcers alerted past signoff time, droned out station breaks, and rejoined the networks.

Abruptly, a tense-voiced New York speaker cut in. "We take you now to London."

Then at 2:32 o'clock from a long ready booth in a London building, the quiet, unhurried, slightly southern drawl of an American Army officer wavered across the Atlantic. "Under the command of General Eisenhower, allied naval forces supported by strong air forces began landing allied armies this morning on the northern coast of France."

That was it. D-Day, H-Hour, had arrived. On all sides of the Forty Acres, many students, studying late for pre-Dead Week exams or awaiting news of the earlier German claims of landings, heard the announcement and began spreading the news. Roommates were rolled out of bed, lights snapped on as fast as word could be screamed down hallways, telephones began to ring, and a rain-drenched Austin came to life.

Radios faintly spluttered with news bulletins. Fifteen-second intervals between items was the maximum wait, and frequently announcers interrupted bulletins with new bulletins. At 3 o'clock, an air-witness description of the first barge to touch shore was broadcast by a returned correspondent, and newsmen in this country followed with a copy that had been written about invasion leaders for over three months.

At 4:30 o'clock, two hours after the announcement, the first real wave of the reaction hit. Home after home around the University was aroused by anonymous, hysterical-voiced women calling to half scream "The invasion is here! The invasion is here!"

Scottish Rite Dormitory girls heard the church bells at 4:40 o'clock and in a matter of minutes lights all over the dorm were shining and radios were busy. At 6 o'clock Monday (June 5th) the bell at the dorm rang accidentally for four minutes and started an excitement-stirring invasion rumor just before mealtime.

The Naval ROTC unit at Andrews Dormitory, though, didn't get the news until 5:30 o'clock when Gordon, limber-lunged newsboy, leaped out of his car shouting "Invasion on ... We're killing them all." In half a minute, lights were shining, halls echoing as ROTC-ees yelped up and down the halls, screaming, reading the stories aloud, and dialing newscasts on every radio.

In fact, it was Gordon, hawking the tabloid size extras, who'd awakened most of the remaining few sleepers near the campus with D-Day news. The tabloid, incidentally, had been ready for sale for two months, except for the final dispatch from invasion headquarters.

As the news spread, though across the campus, reaction from wives, sweethearts, friends and acquaintances of American men in the invasion force told the story of the home front.

Several girls were reported in hysterics for hours after hearing the bulletin. Many wept, others were jubilant, and still other students spent the early hours calling friends to pay off or collect bets on the Invasion Day.

—*THE DAILY TEXAN*
June 7, 1944
reprinted with permission

When Songs Are Sung

(To the tune of *When Day Is Done*)

When songs are sung
By guys we love
To SRD,
It thrills us so
When ere we hear
Your melody.
We left our studies
To listen for awhile.
Your singing voices
Have left us with a
Great big smile.
So, thanks to you for
Serenading us tonight.
Your tunes and thoughts have

Shared with us a feeling bright.
Although it's late and you must go,
Please listen to our plea,
Return to sing again at SRD
—THE SRD SONGBOOK
March 20, 1950

If It's Listening You Are Wanting

(To the tune of Rubin, Rubin, I've Been Thinking)

If it's listening you are wanting,
Fond affection you would like,
Much as we would like to please you
SRD must say: Goodnight (talk)
(Softly whisper—Night night!)
—THE SRD SONGBOOK
March 20, 1950

These two songs were written to sing in appreciation when girls at the dorm were serenaded.

SRD Committee Chosen
to Study House Relations

Members of the new House Relations Committee of Scottish Rite Dormitory are Beverly Stevenson, first floor east; Jean Orr, first floor west; Sue Gottwald, second floor; Glenda Griffitts, third floor; and Renee Merrem, fourth floor.

The committee will serve as a link between the residents and the administration. The first meeting was held Sunday.

Advisers serving on the committee are Sandra Thomas, chairman; Jo Harris, Carolyn Draeger, Sylvia Grider, and Beth Thomas, elected last fall when plans for the committee began.

—*THE DAILY TEXAN*
March 1, 1961
reprinted with permission

Masonic Solons To Be Honored

Governor Price Daniel, along with all legislators who are members of the Masonic order in Texas, will be honored Tuesday at 7 P.M. with a dinner at Scottish Rite Dormitory.

Lee Lockwood* of Waco, Sovereign Grand Inspector General of Scottish Rite Masonry in Texas, will play host to the group of lawmakers.

Two hundred and fifty guests including many outstanding Masons from all over the state are expected to take part in this biennial event.

Governor Daniel will be the principal speaker at the dinner honoring the Texas legislators.

Residents of SRD will be on hand to welcome the guests but will not participate in the dinner.

—THE DAILY TEXAN, March 14, 1961
reprinted with permission

*Lee Lockwood was a member of the board of regents from 1953 to 1959.

Scottish Rite Dorm Feted by Masons

Scottish Rite Dormitory residents, staff, and members of the general board and executive committee were honored with a venison-chili dinner Friday by a group of San Antonio Masons.

Board members and their wives include Senator and Mrs. T. J. Holbrook, Judge and Mrs. Ben Powell, Mr. and Mrs. A. C. Bull, Mr. and Mrs. A. B. Swanson, Mr. and Mrs. Carl Mayer, and L. T. Bellmont.

Hosts were Messrs. and Mesdames P. D. Mathis, J. M. Sears and Harry Brown of San Antonio. They were accompanied by Mrs. Tom Blue, Mrs. Myrtle Burkes and W. B. Jack Ball, and Tom Booth.

Guests were greeted by Miss Neilyn Griggs, president of the dormitory house council. Group singing was accompanied by Miss June Stokes.

—THE DAILY TEXAN
reprinted with permission

Apparently this was an annual event for some years.

Smooth Operator

Until 1968, SRD had a telephone operator who controlled all the calls. Calls were limited to 10 minutes no matter what, and she would come on and tell you, "Time's up," and then "click."

When Ginger lived in the basement and I lived in the maid's quarters, there was a telephone operator who resided down the hall from me. She was very interested in football players and would go out with them late at night. We would see them dropping off their dates at the back door, and then they would pick her up. Don't know where they went or what they did, but she ended up in the Marines.

—JUDY BLACK GOSSLIN, 1966–1970
GINGER MATTHEWS HORTON, 1966–1970

Coeds Contradict Phone Grumblings

The Scottish Rite Dormitory telephone controversy erupted in the Grievance Committee hearing Tuesday with about 50 SRD residents in attendance.

Burke Musgrove, chairman, and the committee heard differing views on the dorm's present switchboard system.

One faction of SRD residents protested against student government interference in the privately-owned dorm's problems. Others complained about the inadequate phone service as a reason for their leaving the dorm.

Mary Ann Wycoff, chairman of All-Campus Advisers and a resident, led a group defending the SRD administration.

"As an individual, I am sick and tired of seeing our staff being harassed by a group of students playing politics," she said.

"Our Board of Directors is working on the problem. Two years ago, I might have jumped on Greg Lipscomb's campaign wagon, but I now understand the problem."

Miss Wycoff had announced at lunch she would attend the meeting and urged residents with differing views to attend also. She claims residents have three outlets other than the Grievance Committee—the Board of Directors, Mrs. F. C. McConnell, administrative head, and their local Masons.

"Don't misunderstand me, this isn't like storming the Bastille. I know we're a thorn in the Student Assembly's side because we didn't come to them with our complaints. They have done all they could to agitate and exploit this issue," she said in a 12-minute speech.

She praised the dorm's swimming pool, air conditioning, new furniture, seated meal service, and landscaping.

"The Board has been working on the problem for three years and I'm certain our Mason fathers and grandfathers will solve it."

"Please leave us alone. We will run our own polls," she concluded. The SRD-packed crowd applauded.

Musgrove moderated the hearing and gave a background of the complaints received. Last spring, his committee received 29 unsigned complaints about the SRD phone [service] on Gripe Day.

During the summer, the issued cooled. The Campus Survey Committee was prohibited Monday from conducting a survey. SRD authorities said the resident roster was obtained under false pretenses.

Richard Troll, a fact-finder from the Grievance Committee, said a private phone would cost $66 for nine months for one resident.

Troll estimated each line is now shared by 21½ residents. He suggested a phone lock to prevent illegal making of long distance calls.

Deposits vary according to a student's credit rating. Usually the company will accept a parent's letter of responsibility and charge no deposit.

Musgrove added that the phone company, if questioned, was obligated to prove an authorized person had made the long distance call.

No agreement has been reached on the total cost of installation, deposit, and monthly charges.

Debate occurred concerning the feasibility of installation of the telephone system. Miss Wycoff claimed the thick walls in SRD would present a problem. Troll claimed the company had estimated no more than normal installation costs.

Miss Wycoff compared the present agitation to the "supposed food 'riots' last spring in SRD. I am tired of seeing our private affairs being spread across the pages of *The Daily Texan*."

Musgrove differed with some details in Miss Wycoff's speech. He said the telephone company would use the same conduits and new drilling would be unnecessary.

"The role of the Grievance Committee is to get the facts, after hearing you, however, I think we may have gone on some false assumptions," Musgrove added.

Greg Lipscomb, president of SA, briefly explained the SA's interest in the private dorm's problem.

SRD Residents Crowd Hearing
... at Grievance Committee—studies telephone problems

"In light of reaction on Gripe Day, I feel it is of concern to the student body in general. The dorm is University-approved. This was our basis for concern. I think they (the Board of Directors and Mrs. McConnell) owed us the courtesy of running the survey.

Oliver Heard, former assemblyman, explained the Centrex system, which operates in the University-approved women's dorms. It is a 24-hour system with one switchboard installed in September 1962.

"I am concerned about the attitude of the resident managers carrying over the patronizing, motherly attitude—this is acceptable to some and unacceptable to others."

Francie Roberts, an SRD resident, said the SA has probably been "meddling."

"The majority of the girls do want private phones and I don't know why the survey was prohibited, but I feel the Masons are doing the best they can."

Nancy Barbee, a former resident, called the phones system "ancient."

Another former resident said 10 out of 18 of her wing moved out.

"We tried to talk to them (Mrs. McConnell and staff) four times last year and were told things were being done about the problem. She related incidents of late delivered flowers and long distance difficulties.

The switchboard closes at 11 P.M. for local calls and 11:30

for long distance calls. Emergency calls are channeled through the night watchman to the dorm after closing. A limit is placed on the length of calls for expediency.

Gina Durette, a senior resident, said the Masons added the swimming pool was [sic] a result of local efforts.

An unidentified SRD counselor reported she had received no complaints about the phone system.

Sue Ellen Allen, a resident, praised Mrs. McConnell for her cooperation.

"On this phone trouble—if a boy doesn't want to give it the good old college try . . ."

Pat Connell, member of the Grievance Committee closed the meeting with a rough draft of the proposal the committee will make.

It concluded:

Any student grievance warrents [sic] the committee's attention.

The purpose is not to dictate solutions, but to give every SRD resident an opportunity to express her feelings.

They are confident that SRD officials will entertain the residents' suggestion and come to a suitable conclusion.

A bill originated by Greg Lipscomb, president of the Students Association, will be considered in the SA's October 8 meeting. On a rotation basis, the SA will meet at SRD that night.

> —DOTTIE LILLARD
> *The Daily Texan*
> September 30, 1964
> reprinted with permission

SRD Coeds: Fill in Blanks
(This will be kept strictly confidential.)

This survey is conducted by Campus Survey Committee. Scottish Rite residents are asked to complete the form and return it to one of the receiving boxes on the corner of Whitis and 24th by the Journalism Building and in front of the Home Economics Building or to the Students' Association [sic] office, Texas Union 323.

Survey for Residents of Scottish Rite Dormitory
Sponsored by the
Students' Association Campus Survey Committee

Length of residence at SRD _____

If not a resident, do you have any opinion? _____

Present Classification _____

Are you satisfied with the current telephone arrangements?
    Yes _____   No_____

Which would you prefer:
    _____ Our own private phone
    _____ The present SRD system

Do you think a private phone would interfere with your studying?   Yes_____   No_____

If you prefer a private phone, would you be willing to pay the following costs which might be shared between roommates:
    Installation fee (one time charge)—$7 plus 10 percent Federal Tax
    Monthly bill $5.50–$6 depending on the number of names listed in the city directory

Deposit (refundable) from 0 to $40 depending on your credit rating. (The deposit is usually disregarded if a letter of guarantee is received from one's parents to assume responsibility.)
    Yes_____   No _____
(A two party line (shared by four girls) would cost approximately $4.50 per month together with a $7 installation fee and deposit if required.)

Do you realize the risk that someone could charge a long distance call to your number?
    Yes_____   No_____

Are you aware that possibly your dormitory room and board bill would be decreased?
    Yes_____   No_____

Name _____

—THE DAILY TEXAN
September 29, 1964
reprinted with permission

Dorm Directors Bar Phone Survey

Authorities of Scottish Rite Dormitory Monday prohibited the Campus Survey Committee, a student government group, to conduct a telephone survey to determine residents' views on the present telephone system in the dormitory.

Mrs. F. C. McConnell, head administrative official, met Monday with Greg Lipscomb, president of the Students' Association, Burke Musgrove, chairman of the Grievance Committee, at Lipscomb's request for approval of the survey. The survey questionnaire was to have been printed Monday night and mailed to SRD residents Tuesday.

Also present at the meeting were Dr. Byron Short and R. A. Mulholland, members of the SRD Executive Committee, and J. C. Hinsley, Grand Senior Warden of the Masons and an Austin attorney.

The survey plan mushroomed this fall after complaints were registered during Gripe Day which was held last spring by the Grievance Committee for students to air complaints against any facet of the University. Twenty-nine of the forms received commented on the telephone system used in Scottish Rite. Each mentioned the need for private telephones.

University-approved women's dormitories switched in September 1962 to Centrex, a 24-hour dial system with one switchboard. Scottish Rite, a privately-owned dormitory for the daughters and relatives of Masons, uses a two-operator switchboard with 12 incoming lines and 10 outgoing lines. Three hundred and seventy-eight woman are served by these lines.

Thursday, a representative of the Campus Survey Committee asked Mrs. McConnell for a roster of SRD residents to be used for committee purposes. Mrs. McConnell stipulated the roster be returned within 24 hours.

A Zerox [sic] copy of the roster was made, and the original then returned within the time period to Mrs. McConnell. Noting that the staple on the original was out of place, Mrs. McConnell called the Campus Survey Committee co-chairman, saying she wanted every copy that had been made of the list.

Lipscomb explained the list had been copied because of the short time period allotted. "We need the names for committee purposes," Lipscomb said.

In Monday's meeting, Mrs. McConnell claimed that the roster was private information and "under no condition shall it be used for anything but that."

"This is a private dormitory and it is run exclusively by the Executive Committee, and if a survey is to be made, they will make it," she continued.

Lipscomb then pointed out that last year's Gripe Day findings revealed the need for a private phone system in SRD. The comments, he said, attacked the closing hour of the switchboard (10:30 P.M. last spring, but since lengthened to 11 P.M. for local and 11:30 for long distance calls), the inconvenience in getting an open line, and the attitude of the switchboard operators.

In a letter dated June 30, 1964, to Judge James W. McClendon, head of the Executive Board of Directors of SRD, Lipscomb said he relayed the results of the campus-wide poll of student dissatisfactions. Ten percent of all comments submitted concerned SRD, principally in the areas of telephones, pool guests, overnight guests, waiters' wages, and the "failure to sign out" rule.

Mulholland said the Board of Directors has been working several years to get a satisfactory telephone system because of past complaints. He denied the validity of the Gripe Day findings because the complaints were unsigned. The Grievance Committee did not allot space for signatures or request them on its forms.

Mrs. McConnell, wife of F. C. McConnell, director of the University Food and Housing, said the contract for a woman to live in SRD was made between the parents and the dormitory.

"Most parents do not want a phone system because it can't be controlled," she said. "One girl would have to agree to pay a phone bill and assume responsibility for long distance calls even if she did not make them."

"Why can't we find out what the girls think?" Lipscomb asked.

"The telephone service is not as we would like for it to be,"

Mrs. McConnell said. "It is possible that in the next few years Southwestern Bell will put us on Centrex." She said the SRD directors would have to approve the change.

Lipscomb said the Board of Directors would hold its annual meeting November 6. His letter to Judge McClendon has been placed on the agenda.

"That is why I need a survey, so I can present it at this meeting," he explained.

Scottish Rite spends more than $10,000 a year operating its present telephone system, not including salaries of the four switchboard operators.

Lipscomb said figures given him by Southwestern Bell showed "the cost of installing private telephones would compare with the present telephone expenses."

Mulholland said, "We are responsible to 55,000 stockholders. The Board will make the decision on the telephones. But you will make no survey in here."

"Campus Survey and Grievance Committees exist," Musgrove replied "to register the demand of students' views. By asking that a survey be taken, the views of the students are on record."

Hinsley said, "If this situation could be washed out and forgotten, and the girls allowed to give forth their views voluntarily, I would say yes to the survey. But not now with all the agitation." He added, "Each SRD resident has the names of the Board members if she wishes to register a complaint."

The Grievance Committee will meet at 3 P.M. Tuesday in Texas Union 302 to consider pending Student Assembly legislation on SRD, Musgove said. Present and former residents of SRD are invited to attend and voice their views.

Under the new policy of meeting in housing units, the Student Assembly will meet October 8 at Scottish Rite Dormitory, Lipscomb said. At that time a bill submitted September 24 concerning areas of student dissatisfaction will be considered.

—THE DAILY TEXAN
September 29, 1964
reprinted with permission

Stump Speakers Sift SA–SRD Situation

"I don't see any girls from SRD out here complaining," a voice noted.

"Well I don't see any girls at all," someone across the circle retorted.

Male students spoke "off the stump" about the telephone situation at Scottish Rite women's dormitory, beginning a five-hour stump speaking session Wednesday.

One co-ed participated in the speaking.

Before the discussion strayed to politics and other issues, about 100 men gathered for the exchange of opinions concerning SRD telephones. Major discussions concerned need for a new phone system at SRD and the right of the Student Assembly to interfere with practices at a private dorm.

The wooden crates on the terrace south of the Main Building for speakers to stand on were used primarily for book rests. Few of the first speakers mounted the "stumps," and then only upon request. By 1:00 P.M. a mixed audience of about 300 persons has gathered as O. B. Hobbs, a speaker familiar from the previous stump-speaking session, again addressed the crowd. "Let's get something to eat," a student, one of the first to gather shortly before noon, said to a friend.

As Hobbs continued, Barry Jagoda climbed atop a stump about 25 feet away.

Jagoda had challenged Hobbs to "talk with facts concerning your support of Goldwater for President."

"This is a free country, and Hobbs can speak if he wants to," Jagoda told the crowd which gathered around him.

Hobbs shortly finished his speaking and joined the group around Jagoda

Politics and the presidential campaign were the primary subjects of discussion throughout the remainder of the speaking.

At 5:00 P.M. a group of about 25 students lingered to "talk politics" by the stumps.

"They're saying the same things over and over," a student observed."

—THE DAILY TEXAN
October 1, 1964
reprinted with permission

Lights in the Dark

The dorm must have been air conditioned in the summer of 1961 because up to that point we used the transoms above our doors.

The dorm was completely full, all the rooms were occupied and in those little bitty rooms by the elevator there on the front hall were trundle beds. We even had girls in bunkbeds in the fifth floor study hall waiting for rooms.

My husband Dan dated several girls at SRD, and he wanted me to be sure and tell you how terrible the phone system was and how after ten minutes they would cut you off and that was it.

During this time they decided to change a few things in the dining hall. One new thing was frozen orange juice. We were all used to the fresh squeezed, and when the change occurred we had a rebellion that made the pages of the *Daily Texan*.

Hurricane Carla hit in the fall of 1961. Mother and Daddy brought me down, moved me into the dorm and then they turned around and went home. They were in traffic because so many people were fleeing the coast. That night they drew water in all the bathtubs at SRD because they were afraid our electricity would go out and sure enough it did, but SRD had a generator, as did UT. It was a strange feeling because all of Austin was dark except for UT and SRD.

—Sylvia Hulsey West
1960–1964

SRD Will Be Real Cool

The first phase of the architects' plans for a projected $300,000 air conditioning of the Scottish Rite Dormitory was approved by the SRD board of directors Saturday.

Mrs. F. C. McConnell, general director of the dormitory, says that the second phase, including bids for the work, will be presented at the June 1 meeting of the board.

—The Daily Texan
April 11, 1962
reprinted with permission

SRD Waiter Says Asked to Resign

Dormitory Claims Student Behind Bad Food Protest

A Scottish Rite Dormitory waiter said Thursday he had been asked to resign because of his involvement in the residents' protests of the food.

Paul Van Slyke, employed at the Masonic-owned dormitory for approximately two years, said Mrs. F. C. McConnell, head administrative official, felt he was responsible for recent protests about the food.

Mrs. McConnel describing Slykes as a "fine boy," said she would not call it a dismissal, but an "adjustment in personnel."

Waiters "Bawled Out"

He said waiters were "bawled out" Wednesday night by Mrs. McConnell. "Scottish Rite employs approximately 25 student waiters," Mrs. McConnell said, "who receive meals as their pay."

Tuesday and Wednesday the *Texan* received telephone calls from residents who refused to identify themselves, saying that walk-outs were planned at dinners.

"Mrs. McConnell spoke to all the waiters, and looking directly at me, said the problem of the rumored walk-outs rests in the leadership of the waiters," Slykes said.

Approximately 350 women live in the women's dormitory.

Slykes and Mrs. Doris Patterson, food production manager, who could not be reached for comment, claimed he had stirred up most of the trouble. He said the manager told him he "was arrogant and could not admit his mistakes" and asked for his resignation.

The dormitory official said there had been more than the usual amount of complaints about the food, but attributed it to Mrs. Patterson's newness at the job.

"It will probably take her a little time to adjust to the girl's appetites and tastes," Mrs. McConnell said.

Plans No Dismissals

A senior electrical engineering student, Slykes said he thought it was a problem of "too many bad meals served in a short time period."

"It certainly was accelerated by the fact that during one of the noon meals a spider fell out of a girl's sandwich," Slykes said.

Mrs. McConnell flatly denied any such incident. She said the dormitory, in service for 43 years, served "excellent" food.

A resident who requested her name not be used said the bread served during "the meal was so stale it crumbled, and two tables piled sandwiches on a plate and sent them back to the kitchen."

Tension Cause

"It is only natural for everyone not to agree on every item of food served," Mrs. McConnell said. "Tensions of campus life can be readily expressed through comments on living conditions."

Threats of residents taking action have been circulating for several weeks. Monday night's menu consisted of roast beef with corn and tomatoes mixed as the vegetable.

Tuesday's lunch was potato soup, cole slaw, and cheddar cheese sandwiches, rolls, stuffed eggs, corn chips, crackers, ripe olives, and pineapple salad with cottage cheese.

Residents reportedly have been keeping lists of meals served and plan to write home about the situation. To live in SRD, a student must be sponsored by a member of the Masonic order.

Mrs. McConnell, at SRD since 1950, said she could not remember any recent dismissals and "certainly" was not planning anymore.

Milvern Harrell, senior pharmacy student, handed over a letter of resignation to Mrs. McConnell Thursday night at dinner and walked out during the meal.

Harrell, when questioned whether he would serve Friday, answered, "If I'm asked to." Then in answer to a question if he would be asked to serve then, he said, "no comment."

Eat in Silence

Students ate their dinner Thursday in silence to protest the waiter's dismissal, said a resident, who refused to give her name.

Patty Stephens, cochairman of the Student Government Grievance Committee, announced Thursday night that the committee will take up the issue at its meeting at 4 P.M. Tuesday in Texas Union.

—SHARON SHELTON
The Daily Texan
November 22, 1963
reprinted with permission

SRD Receives Bust of Masonic Leader

A bust of Lee Lockwood, Sovereign Grand Inspector General in Texas, was presented to Scottish Rite Dormitory Tuesday night at the Biennial Appreciation Dinner in honor of Masons in the Legislature.

Former governor Price Daniel received the bust for SRD from Leon Shaw of Dallas.

Bryant Baker, sculptor, created the Lockwood bust, which was a gift of Dallas Scottish Rite Masons.

The dinner was held in the Scottish Rite Dormitory dining room in honor of the 300 members present. Lockwood presided at the dinner and Texas Supreme Court Associate Justice Zollie Coffer Steakley Jr. gave the after dinner speech. Of the 300 members present, 11 were State Senators and 56 were State Representatives.

The Masons began their day with a seminar at 10 A.M. at the Austin Scottish Rite Temple to discuss the events of the centennial year for Texas Masons.

"The centennial year has been actively engaged thus far. We announced at the seminar plans for a new state library and museum to be built in Waco."

—THE DAILY TEXAN
March 29, 1967
reprinted with permission

This bust is mentioned as a "statue of an old army man" in one of the following ghost stories.

Is SRD Really a "Haunted House"?

All those stories couldn't possibly be true ... or could they?

Is SRD really haunted?

Here at Scottish Rite Dormitory, there is a sense of safety and security that comforts us as we walk through the door. We know there are lots of sweet people looking out for us, like the RAs at the front desk, the maintenance men in the office by the back door, and ... ghosts? Considering that we live in a building that opened in the 1920s, it's pretty reasonable to think that we may not be the only residents that occupy the halls of SRD. Of course, all the stories that we've heard can't possibly be true ... or can they? You decide yourself.

Spooky Situation #1: It was several years ago, and all the girls were home celebrating Thanksgiving with their families. Only a few of the staff remained at the dorm. Late one night, after everyone had gone to bed, one of the ladies heard loud, uncontrollable sobs coming from 1st East. She said that after a while of contemplating what to do, she finally decided to get out of bed and see if she could help, even though she knew there shouldn't have been anyone else on that side of the dormitory. After walking up the stairs and looking around on the floor, she just couldn't seem to figure out where it was coming from. Finally, she walked back to her room and shut the door, and at that very moment, the crying ceased.

Spooky Situation #2: Another strange occurrence happened after the death of a beloved SRD administrator. After her funeral, her portrait was hung in the hallway along with all the others. That night, a loud thud was heard by one of the house mothers. The next morning, she awoke to find that the picture had mysteriously crashed to the floor. After talking amongst themselves, one of the staff members recalled that she had always said she didn't want her picture hung anywhere in the building. However, they didn't feel right by leaving her out, and so they decided they must have made a mistake while hanging it, and put it back in its place. That night, there was another thud—the portrait had fallen again! They hung it back up, and it has remained ever since.

Spooky Situation #3: Late one night, an SRD girl was studying for a test on the 5th floor, which was decorated with a bronze statue of an old army man. It was pretty late when she decided to go downstairs to bed. She was on her way out when all of a sudden, she screamed and dropped her books. To this day, she swears that his eyes moved, and that he was watching her as she walked out the door. The statue has since been removed.

Spooky Situation #4: Several years ago, a few girls were coming in late and realized they had forgotten their keys. The house mother on duty came to unlock their doors, and on her way back to her room, she saw a man, wearing a suit and hat, and holding a cigar, sitting on a couch in the lobby. Strangely, he looked just like a respected Austinite who had died a few months earlier. She looked away and went straight to her room, never looking back to see who really was the midnight visitor. Could it have been a hallucination? Maybe, but a closer look at surveillance tapes revealed a masculine figure that seemed to appear and disappear repeatedly throughout the night. He hasn't been around since.

We hope you have enjoyed reading these stories as much as we enjoyed researching and writing about them. Until next time, lock your doors girls, and have fun on Halloween!

—CHELSEA BELOTE
The Scribbling Squirrel
October 2006

Spirited Cooking

There have been many times I have heard someone entering through the back kitchen entrance, the door closing and footsteps down the stairs, but then no one is there. Also, objects in the kitchen have been moved from one location to another without anyone "owning up to it." Rumor has it that there used to be an older male cook who would go out into the back of the dorm to wring the necks of the chickens that he was preparing for dinner. Now, whether or not it is his spirit still lingering around, or somebody else's, I do not know, but there is definitely someone present.

—Tracy Mussey
Food Service Director
1991–present

Mary Frances Crosby

My freshman year (1975) I was in 357 (3rd East), and down the hall lived Bing Crosby's daughter, Mary Frances Crosby, who turned 16 that fall. She got in early because of private tutoring. Her mother was a UT alumnus.

Mary Frances, at UT only one year, was in the chorus for the *Oklahoma* production. Freshmen were not given speaking parts. She joined Tri-Delta and went on to become famous appearing in the TV show *Dallas* as Kristin, Sue Ellen's little sister who shot J. R. Ewing.

—Jamie Gillians Turner
1975–1978

Interesting People

There were many interesting people at the dorm. Of course we had our dorm administrator, Mrs. Townes. Probably better known to us were our "house mothers," Mrs. Evans and Mrs. Pruitt. Mrs. Evans lived on the 1st floor and Mrs. Pruitt up on 3rd. These ladies were pretty unflappable. I remember when the Fijis stormed through the ground level entrance on the west side of the building. I believe there were one or two streakers. I think one of these fellows either jumped or was thrown into the lap of a girl watching TV in the Rec Room. After it was all over, we asked Mrs. Evans what she thought of the streakers. In her Boston accent she said, "Well, deah, when you've had a husband and two sons . . ."

Who could forget our night watchmen! They were supposed to walk around with the R.A.s as we locked up for the night. We had some extremes. There was Mr. Giles, the retired Marine, and then there was Mo. I am sure many people remember Mo. He was a good fellow, but I'm sure he spent more than his fair share of time on the Drag. He had that "always needs a shave" look before it became so popular.

And of course we had our wonderful maids! What other dorm was so lucky! Our maid was Minnie.* I heard that she retired just a few years ago.

—ANNA HOLMGREN
1976–1980

*Minnie retired in 2006 at the age of 81, having worked at the dorm for 30 years.

Still Cookin'

Amie: What do you think about the waiters?

Pauline: They are really great, but they are funny. Some of them are really, really funny.

Amie: What is something funny that they do?

Ethel: Well, for one thing the guys come in and a lot of times don't have the hot pads, and they try to pick up the steam table trays, and they say, "Ooh it's hot! Why didn't you tell me?" One of them did it last night. He dropped it, and I said, "You'll never forget, right?" He said, "No, you're right." But we enjoy the guys; they make our day and night.

Amie: What are some other funny things that the waiters have done?

Ethel: One time they brought the potatoes out that weren't even done.

Pauline: And a few guys have taken a whole can of food and dropped it on the floor.

Pauline: They have changed the milk, milk has been all over the dining room, and I know a couple of guys who have done that here lately. They were new and were learning how to change the milk and didn't get it quite right the first time. One guy had it all over his shirt. He had to leave and change clothes because he had milk everywhere.

Amie: A waiter from the 1960s told me that if they dropped the china they had to pay for it. Is that still true?

Pauline: Well, we mess with the waiters now and then and tell them if they break something, that's $4.25 and that was $3.00 for the bowl you just dropped.

Amie: Are the waiters on time?

Pauline: The waiters are always late, and some of them don't even show up sometimes.

Amie: Anything the girls do that bothers you?

Ethel: The girls make off with the silverware. The silverware is a really big problem here. Ya'll didn't do that when ya'll was here.

Amie: Well, it did happen some, but the old china was a bigger problem."

Pauline: This china is still a big problem.

Amie: Now, you've both worked here 25 years?

Pauline: Ethel has been here 29 years and I just made 25.

Amie: What is different about the waiters and girls from when you came to now?

Ethel: To me, it's just a few girls that will say hi, but lately if they don't know you, you'll smile, and they'll smile, but eventually they will get to know you. If they don't know you, they won't say anything. The few that I know are real nice.

Amie: Are the waiters still fraternity boys?

Together: Yes, for the most part.

Amie: Now come on. I know there has to be some more good stories about the waiters!

Pauline: The waiters keep things to themselves. They don't really let us get in on it because they know if we know, we're going to tease them about it.

Ethel: Some of them are really sweet and kind of shy.

Amie: A waiter from the past told me a story about a lady from the kitchen chasing one of the waiters with a knife. Do you remember who that was?

Together: It wasn't me. (*Pauline*). (*Pauline to Ethel*) Did you chase somebody with a knife?

Amie: Do the waiters still play the guitar at Christmas time?

Ethel: No, not any more. They have the talent to do that, but they don't.

Pauline: This year we had a Santa Claus and an elf, though.

Amie: Do you like working here in general?

Pauline: Sometimes is gets hectic, but most of it I have enjoyed.

Amie: What about you, Ethel?

Ethel: Sometimes it be hectic. It all depends on what Tracey has on the menu, and it can be overwhelming, but I've managed to get it done.

Amie: When I came to live here, I heard a lot of stories about not getting in your way, Ethel. "Don't get in Ethel's way or she'll get ya!" Are those true?

Pauline: I think that story still goes. Her legend precedes her.

Ethel: You see that boy (a waiter) over there looking at us. He came up to me when he first started working here and said, "I've heard a lot of stories about you."

Ethel: If I have an attitude, I don't mean to, but I just don't put up with anything. Last night Zach was getting something out of the steamer, and I jokingly told him not to drop it, and the look of fear he gave me! I'll never forget that.

Amie: Any of the other kitchen employees do anything funny?

Pauline: What did we used to call Ray (the baker) because he was so messy? We saw a (work place) video upstairs where the main character's name was, Dirty something because his apron was so dirty. Ray would have flour all over his apron, all over his shoes, all over the floor, the walls and he'd say, "I'm a baker, and you can tell I'm working because flour is everywhere."

Amie: I really loved the strawberry bread and still make it at home sometimes.

Pauline: I made so many loaves of strawberry bread and lemon bread and apple pie cake and oatmeal cake, I don't even want to see none of that it was on the menu so much!

Amie: What are some things you are glad you no longer have to make?

Ethel: I'm glad I don't have to make dumplin's anymore. Dumplin's. I tell you what. I used to have to roll that dough and cut it out. Having to roll it out and cut it. That was time consuming for this many girls. I'm so glad I don't have to do that anymore. And shish-ka-bob, I don't like to make them either!

Amie: What are some of the specialty dishes that you still make?

Pauline: Still make crepes, baby-back ribs, King Ranch Casserole, and we still have our famous CCB's!

Ethel: Fried chicken and we have those twice-baked potatoes. They eat those like they are drinking water.

Amie: Anything that you miss that they don't make anymore?

Pauline: I didn't eat dessert when I made it. There was just too much of it. I couldn't eat it. But I can eat a lot of it now that somebody else is making it! It tastes a lot better because someone else is making it.

—ETHEL SIMMS
Kitchen Staff, 29 years

—PAULINE FRESCH
Kitchen Staff, 25 years

Wanted . . .

Spoons, ice tea glasses, china, sugar bowls.

Scottish Rite Dormitory's having a stealing problem. Numerous and valuable pieces of tableware are constantly being removed from the dining room. Stainless steel spoons are now being used since some of SRD's silver is being transformed into spoon rings. Seventy ice tea glasses were removed within a two-week period.

Have you forgotten and walked out of the dining room drinking your tea? If so, SRD would like its stolen goods returned. Boxes will be placed on each end of the halls. Spoons, glasses, and other serviceware are asked to be placed in these containers. No questions will be asked. Please return any article you find.

—DUBE'S DISPATCH
RA Newsletter, 1975

Becky Shannon Eaddy, who lived at SRD during this time confirms that indeed rings were being made from the silver spoon handles from SRD and some even appeared for sale at the Renaissance Market on the Drag.

Alumnae Association and SRD Reunion 1990

I lived in SRD from 1976-1980. When I lived in SRD, I had many friends in the staff and stayed in touch with them after graduation by stopping by when I was in Austin. I returned to live in Austin in 1990.

A month before I returned I stopped by to talk with the staff, and Mrs. Adele Millen (SRD Administrator, 1983–91) and Mr. Roy Mulholland (President of the SRD Board of Directors) asked me to start an Alumnae Association. Note: Mr. Mulholland had been on the Board for some time and was on the Board when I lived in SRD. In 1990 SRD was only 40% to 50% occupied.

I agreed to get an Alumnae Association started and have a reunion that coming football season. I had no idea what I had signed on for. I asked what the budget was and was told there was no budget, but I had to clear things through Mrs. Millen and Mr. Mulholland.

I moved to Austin in June and started researching on July 4, 1990. That July 4th my options were to start the SRD research or go to a Willie Nelson picnic. I opted for air-conditioning. I got all the rosters from the archives and with lots of help from Pam Archer, the SRD Librarian, and RAs and other SRD residents, we cross-referenced years and made a list of SRD residents from 1920 to 1990.

In all this research I discovered that the lady who lived in the same house I grew up in and the daughters of my next-door neighbor lived in SRD in the '40s. (Coming from a town of 2,687, that's a big deal.) This research took many evenings and weekends. I would go directly from work to SRD and go through the rosters until 10 or 11 P.M. Many pounds were lost. The decades of '30s, '40s, '50s, '70s, and '80s were well organized. I do not know why the rosters from the '60s were not all there. This could be why we do not have a big showing of '60s alumnae at the reunions.

After a list of SRD residents was assembled with maiden

names and home address while at SRD, I contacted the Texas Exes to cross-reference. The Texas Exes was a big help in converting maiden names to married names and finding current addresses. Also, I got a list of every Texas Exes group and its president and sent each Texas Ex a letter with a flier about the 1st reunion and asked them to announce it at their monthly meetings.

I contacted an ad/art person; worked with her and got an ad prepared for and printed in the September 1990 *Alcalde*. I contacted people at Memorial Stadium and the Cotton Bowl and put announcements about the reunion on the Jumbotron. The 1st invitations were large postcards of SRD sent to every one on our SRD/Texas Exes roster. Many invitations were returned with forwarding information, and many parents forwarded the invitations to their daughters.

The 1990 reunion had a 10:00 A.M. coffee and a party at 6:00 P.M. A piano player was hired for the evening party. I heard him at the Melrose Hotel in Dallas and thought we would enjoy hearing him. He agreed to fly down and play if SRD paid for him and his wife to stay at the Four Seasons Hotel in Austin. I had a friend who worked in promotions at the Four Seasons and worked out a deal. At the first reunion I found a party picture business to take pictures, get them developed and back to SRD in one hour and posted them on a board for people to see and order pictures. SRD has all those pictures. The first reunion had current SRD residents hired to be babysitters. The turnout for the 1990 reunion was more than 600, and people were still at SRD at midnight. A good time was had by all.

After the reunion, Pam Archer, the SRD Librarian, and I wrote a newsletter containing pictures of the reunion and asked for volunteers to help. Sheila Kerr Sorgee (1969–'73) volunteered, and from that time on she has been doing a lot of the heavy lifting in the SRD Alumnae Association. Two other early volunteers who helped are Myra Lee (Duffer) Summers (BA '43) and Margaret Fairbairn Legett (BBA '44).

SRD is now full and has a waiting list. I think the Alumnae Association reunions and its word of mouth have helped. I have been an Honorary Member on the SRD Advisory Committee and Board of Directors since 2002. When I go to the Board and Advisory Committee meetings, I remember how "old" those men looked when I was a resident. I still feel like I'm a resident and sure hope I don't look as "old" as they did when I lived at SRD.

—KATHY KEILS
1976–1980

Yesterday or Yesteryear?
Chances Are Your Reunion's Near

For those of you who've dreamed of reliving those golden days at the Scottish Rite Dormitory—with the beautiful holiday dinners, afternoons by the pool, and the excitement of the Spring Formal—your time has come.

On Saturday, October 20, at 10 A.M. Scottish Rite Dormitory will host a reunion for all SRD alumnae. Reunion chair Kathy Keils, BBA '81, is trying to collect the names of former residents, including maiden and current names, year of graduation, addresses, and telephone numbers. Please contact her at 210 W. 27th Street, Austin 78705, or phone 512-476-9131.

—ALCALDE
September/October 1990
reprinted with permission

Scottish Rite Dormitory Celebrates
75 Successful Years

At the Scottish Rite Dormitory, traditions from eras gone by are clung to as the impending 21st century is embraced.

After 75 years, Scottish Rite Dormitory is still rich with tradition and proud of its history. In the early 1900s, when the University of Texas at Austin didn't have sufficient housing for young women, the Master Masons of Texas recognized the need and decided to do something about it.

The year was 1920. Flapper dresses were on the verge of becoming the latest fashion, and the Charleston dance would soon sweep the nation. Under President Wilson, we had won the war to make the world "safe for democracy." Women gained the right to vote with the ratification of the 19th Amendment, and the stock market would shortly begin to skyrocket. The "roar" that America would forever associate with the "Dollar Decade" was on the brink of blasting.

This was the year that Samuel P. Cochran, 33, the executive head of Scottish Rite Masonry in Texas, began his project of building a dormitory suitable for young ladies attending the university. In order for construction to begin, Cochran asked the Scottish Rite Bodies of Texas to donate the necessary funds.

The response of Masons across the state was overwhelmingly generous. One million dollars was raised over a period of two years. Thus, the dormitory opened its doors to university women in the fall of 1922 completely debt free. From that year on, Scottish Rite Dormitory has been "the only one of its kind in the world," according to Sam E. Hilburn, 33, Chairman, Board of Directors of the dormitory. From the chandeliers, oriental rugs, and gourmet food to the computer labs, aerobics classes, aquatic center and hot tub, Scottish Rite Dormitory combines the elegance of an era gone by with modern-day amenities.

SRD, as the dorm is affectionately called, was built on seven acres one block north of the University of Texas, Austin, in order to provide the utmost convenience for its residents. A profusion of oak trees, planted almost eight decades ago, now provides the front lawn with a canopy of shade for the young women to enjoy and a home for countless squirrels. Strolling along the sidewalk that leads to the main entrance, one is granted a glimpse of the columned, red brick edifice, characteristic of the Georgian architectural design, that stands within the trees.

While sitting in the lavish parlor room, one could easily mistake the surroundings for a five-star hotel. The twenty-foot ceiling, pink velvet couches, and antique tables are only a few items that set SRD apart. Portraits of past house mothers and administrators adorn the walls. Chairs covered with tapestries sewn by former residents have now become cherished memorabilia, and the baby grand piano patiently awaits an opportunity to feature Gershwin and Bach.

Not only is SRD physically unlike conventional college dormitories, it prides itself on traditions that endure to this day. One of the most popular events is the annual Christmas celebration. Residents compete in a decorating contest to see which hall can be the most creative. Then the festivities continue with Christmas dinner, caroling, and a visit by Santa. Also, a Valentine's dance is given as well as barbecues and shrimp boils throughout the year.

In keeping with tradition, males are restricted from access to residents' halls until the weekend from one o'clock in the afternoon to six o'clock in the evening. Also, Sunday dinner is formal style. Residents are served by waiters who are also university students. However, the rules didn't use to be so lenient. Regulations enforced in the early days would most likely scare the '90s woman away. Here is an example from the original rules:

Three engagements a week are allowed; the young lady is expected to confer with her chaperon before making an engagement, and to return promptly at the close of all entertainments. Taking meals at hotels or at downtown restaurants is a violation of propriety ... Young men may call on Friday evenings, Sunday afternoons and evenings, leaving at 10:30. Two couples may take a short automobile ride in the daytime. No night rides unchaperoned or on country roads are to be allowed.

Though this is quite a change from today's mores, SRD's purpose remains the same as stated in the original corporate charter: "to surround residents during their university course with a wholesome, moral environment, and with the associations of home life, in addition to its comforts and conveniences."

As SRD celebrates its 75th anniversary, traditions from eras gone by are still clung to as the impending 21st century is embraced. Being a longtime admirer and one-time resident of the dormitory, I think Mr. Cochran and all the Masons who contributed to this structure would be proud to see how it has withstood the adversities of time and remained

a cherished and beloved home for aspiring young women today.
—ASHLEY ALLCORN

SRD is in the National Register of Historic Places! The listing is:

Texas, Travis County,
Scottish Rite Dormitory,
210 W. 27th St., Austin
98000404, Listed 4/23/98

Rules, Rules, Rules

You Have To Be Mighty Smart—

- ♥ To get a ride down in the elevator.
- ♥ To get to come in after 11 o'clock and not sign a late slip.
- ♥ To get "seconds" on dessert at dinner.
- ♥ To borrow your roommate's last towel.
- ♥ To make a midnight show.
- ♥ To get breakfast after 8:15 o'clock in the morning.
- ♥ To come down to meals with your hair rolled up.
- ♥ To appear in the lobby floor without hose on.
- ♥ To talk over the phone after 8 o'clock at night.
- ♥ To bring up food to your room.
- ♥ To play your radio very loud after 8 o'clock at night.
- ♥ To get an outside line right after lunch or dinner.
- ♥ To hang your washing in the windows.
- ♥ To holler at your roommate from the window when she's out smoking.

—if you stay at SRD
—THE SARDINE, 1940

Locked Out

I must say that of all the dorms at UT, this one was the most beautiful and friendly, as were the girls who lived there. Advisors, "mothers," and friends surrounded you every day.

My most vivid memory is my fear of the night watchman. In reality he was a nice man who let girls in who had broken curfew, but I imagined him to carry a ball with spikes, which he used to punish girls who dared come home late.

My first night at the dorm I became confused about the time and arrived after the doors had been locked. Overcome with the stress of having to confront the back door "ogre" so early in my tenure, I wet my pants.

—BETH BAKER QUALIA
1974–1975

Afternoon Tea and Celebrities

I arrived at SRD, which was referred to as "The Bastille," from Pecos, Texas, in the fall of 1954 a real West Texas girl. The strict rules actually benefited me, and I made my best grades that first semester when I had to be in each night at 8:30 except for late-night weekends when it was 10:30 or 11:00 P.M.

One of my funniest memories happened during my first "tea." Ms. Allison was pouring and asked if I would like lemon or milk. Unknowing, I replied "both." Curdled and ugly result! When I returned for another cup, I told her I would like it "straight." Not too ladylike but a real West Texas term!

As if fancy teas weren't enough, when Charlton Heston attended dinner that fall of 1955, standing tall above all us coeds, eyes wide, interested and attentive, I thought this would be a regular occurrence and celebrities would often visit SRD!

—Pat Parker Freeburg
1954–1958

Family Style

We had seated meals three times a day—two lunch periods, and the evening meal. I usually ate at the first lunch at 12:10 P.M., depending on my school schedule, although I preferred the second lunch at 1:10 P.M. It was smaller.

When the first dinner bell would ring, we would go down the wide, sweeping stairs for meals and line up outside the closed doors of the dining hall. Our waiters had usually set the tables for us and stood ready for the second dinner bell to ring ten minutes later. When the second bell rang, the doors would open and the girls would rush in, trying to get to the table of their preferred waiters. We all stood behind our chairs until the members of the head table came in. The waiters stood with their hands folded in front of them, showing respect. The members of the head table came in after all the girls had entered and were standing, waiting.

The head table included Mrs. McConnell, all the dorm

moms and various other guests. When the members of the head table were in place, the waiters took turns saying grace. Here is one prayer I memorized that Grover McMains said every time: "Give us grateful hearts, our Father, for these and all thy blessings, and make us mindful of the needs of others. Amen." After the prayer, we all sat down. I can hear to this day the sound of the chairs scraping on the floor and the voices of the girls chattering away.

The waiters would go and get the plates from the kitchen, carrying them on huge, silver trays. They deposited the trays on a holder beside the table, and set the food out for us to pass family style. We could ask for seconds of the vegetables, but not usually seconds on meat. Then the waiters would remove the serving dishes, our plates, and silverware and carry the trays back into the kitchen. They returned seconds later with dessert. Our favorite dessert was Chocolate Crumble Balls. The first time I ever ate Gingerbread with Lemon Icing was at SRD. I also loved that dessert.

—JANE ARCHER FEINSTEIN
1964–1966, 1967

No Pants Allowed

When I was living at SRD in 67-68, things were more "proper." We could not come into the front room or the dining hall in our slacks. When it was time to get ready for dinner, we would put our skirts on over our shorts.

Right now standing here talking to you I'm feeling pretty guilty wearing my slacks in the front room. SRD definitely left an impression on me.

—CAROL CLANTON RASCO
1967–1968

Fashion Forward

The wonderful sit-down dinners and foods were always a treat. However, every now and then, having to be in the dining hall before the last bell rang was a challenge. This was definitely the case one December afternoon. My room-mates, friends, and I decided to do our Christmas shopping before going home for the holidays. We returned to SRD just as the last bell was about to ring. I knew I didn't have time to get to my room, change into a dress and get back down to the dining hall before the last bell. Using my best problem-solving skills, I ducked into a service room, took off my slacks, and proceeded to my table wearing my pants coat. Thanks to the days of the mini skirt, no one knew the difference.

—PEGGY LOWRIE
1968–1969

Handbook for SRD Girls

On retiring at night the exhausted maiden should set her alarm clock—or some one else's—at least fifteen minutes earlier than she expects to arise. These fifteen minutes will give her time enough to get back to sleep before time for her eight o'clock classes.

Upon rising she should put on her roommate's newest dress—evening dresses excluded—and rush to school.

She should never reach her eight o'clock classes on time—although if she is a freshman her promptness to classes is excusable.

As soon as she has gotten as much out of the class as she wants, she should leave and go to the Drag.

There she should meet her "big moment" and remain with him until he can no longer put up with her.

When he has deserted her, she should go to her next class, if she has any more—unless she has something else she had rather do.

As soon as she has gone to all the classes which she cares about visiting that day, she should return to the dormitory to await the "mess call"—the radio has very good programs all morning.

After lunch, if she feels like it, she may page through her lessons, but if she finds herself getting bored, she can put off studying until *manana* and go out.

If her roommate isn't in when she leaves, she should call down the hall to someone to answer her buzzes.

If she so desires, she may leave her date book with the chump, thus being assured that all requests for dates will be accepted immediately. In this way the young man will not have time to think over having a date with her. It is not wise to be too sure.

If, when she returns, the date book is still blank, she should if possible, get herself a date. Failing in this, she can either go to bed or listen to the radio.

She, perhaps, will do neither, but we will not hold it against her if she does not accept this advice—she has to dig her own grave, we've already dug ours.

—*THE SARDINE*
Volume 11, 1933

The Witching Hour

When I lived at SRD from 1964–1966, there was a 12:00 A.M. curfew at which time you were expected to be inside the building. At 10 minutes till, the light flashed. At five minutes till, the light flashed again. At 1 minute till, the light flashed, and the door began to close, and if you did not get in the door, you were locked out. Mrs. McConnell, the resident director, locked that door and that was it. No, ifs, ands, or buts.

—BETTY CHALFONT
1964–1966

Dating Protocol

In 1964, we had phones in our rooms, but our calls came in from the outside through a switchboard. Mrs. LeBorde was the switchboard operator. Any visitor or date would come in and ask Mrs. LeBorde to call us down from our rooms to the front. Our visitors would wait in the front foyer until we came down from our rooms. Then, we had to sign in and out at the front desk.

Our curfews were 11:00 P.M. on weeknights and midnight

on Friday and Saturday nights. Sunday through Thursday, I signed out of the dorm by 7 P.M., went straight to the UGL (Undergraduate Library) to study. I walked back to sign in by 10 P.M.

On weekends, if we had dates, sometimes we would pull up outside the dorm and park until they blinked the lights on the front porch. Those blinking lights meant we had five minutes to get in the dorm before we would be late for curfew. I never missed a curfew.

—JANE ARCHER FEINSTEIN
1964-1966, 1967

UT Column

Farewell embraces were short and sweet on the steps of Scottish Rite Dormitory Sunday morning.

The reason the male students didn't linger was in the form of a five-foot coachwhip snake, which dangled from a tree near the dorm entrance. Jan Keng visited her home in Sonora this weekend and accidentally ran over the reptile enroute. She couldn't resist the temptation of bringing it back.

SRD residents set a record breaking pace at saying goodnight.

—CHARLIE SMITH
The Daily Texan, May 16, 1961
reprinted with permission

Kiss and Tell

A guy was kissing his girlfriend outside, saying goodnight, and a maintenance man known as "Tops," but really named Ralph, walked up behind him. Standing like a foot away from his ear he said, "What do you think you're doing?"

The guy jumped like three feet in the air.

"You don't have permission to kiss these girls. These girls are *my* girls!"

—HALEY WHITCOMB
2006–present

Trays and Ice

In the winter of 1973 we had a fairly heavy snowstorm. The next day, some SRD residents borrowed trays from the dining room and used them as sleds to go down the hill behind the Presbyterian Seminary dorm. Apparently the seminary students were doing the same thing, having borrowed trays from their dining room, also. If I remember correctly, the SRDians got in a bit of trouble for "borrowing" the trays.

—ANONYMOUS
1972–1975

Follow the Rules, or Else!

I especially remember the smoking lounge at the end of the 3rd floor hall. There you could meet your friends to smoke cigarettes (not allowed in the rooms), eat junk food (also not allowed in the room), and play bridge all night long on Friday and Saturday after your date brought you back to the dorm. Forty-eight years later, none of us smoke, most of us eat junk food, some of us play bridge, and a special group of us still get together to celebrate the friendships made in the "smokers."*

Although we could smoke at the dorm there were plenty of other rules SRD had and enforced. After all, we were young ladies whose families and sponsors expected us to live up to the highest standards. Curfew was 11:00 P.M. Sunday through Thursday and 12:45 A.M. on Friday and Saturday. You were to sign out of the dorm even when you went home for a holiday.

Forgetting to do this one Easter weekend, my mother called Ms. McConnell, Scottish Rite Dorm Director, as soon as I arrived home to explain the situation. Was I ever surprised on my return to SRD to find out I was grounded to the dorm for a week from 6:00 P.M. to 6:00 A.M. for failure to sign out. Lesson learned: accepting responsibility for my actions!

—KATHLEEN EDWARDS SIMPSON
1958–1961

*The smoking lounges or "smokers" were rooms set aside for smoking and socializing. They were meant to keep girls from sitting on the

SRD steps and smoking in public. These rooms later became TV lounges and when I lived at SRD (1993–1997), smoking was banned, and you could always see a cluster of girls around the back steps smoking.

Don't Mess with Patsy!

Mrs. Patsy Shurr was the dorm receptionist from 1990–2002 and was quite a character. She dearly loved most of the girls but could be a force to be reckoned with if you crossed her. Parking in the upper RA and staff spaces was always an issue with her. Some girls just never seemed to understand that the spots had painted numbers and the word "Staff" for a reason.

During a particularly bad spell of "illegal" parking, Patsy arrived at work to find a resident's car in her spot. After locating a place for her car, she marched directly into the dorm and cross-referenced the girl by her license plate number. Finding that she lived on 2nd Central, Patsy proceeded to phone her room numerous times. Getting no answer she decided to visit the girl's room. Arriving at the offender's room, she found the door ajar. She knocked and quietly opened the door. The girl was fast asleep in bed and awoke with a great start when Patsy addressed her and shook her arm. After the girl recovered from her fright, she promptly moved her car and probably never parked in Patsy's spot again.

To those of us who were juniors and seniors with assigned parking spots at the time, we took great pleasure in knowing our privileged parking spaces were protected by Pasty.

—AMIE STONE KING
1993–1997

It's Personal

Granny Brat

Mary Catherine Pennington was the Resident Director/ Dorm Mother from 1992–1998. She was a precious woman except at 3:00 A.M. when you were locked out of your room. Some girls chose to sleep in their friend's rooms or in the hall rather than wake her because there was always a lecture involved and she could be scary.

Mrs. Pennington liked to say in a very joking manner that we were all brats and began to address me in particular as Brat. In private I had begun calling her Granny Brat but was not brave enough to say it to her face. My yet-to-be husband Matt was an SRD waiter and often ran into Mrs. Pennington while at the dorm. He had heard me call her Granny Brat numerous times in conversations, and one night as he was waiting for me in the office visiting with her, he addressed her as Granny Brat. I almost fainted. She looked stunned for a minute and then laughed. He had no idea that I didn't actually call her that to her face. Of course, from then on she was Granny Brat (GB for short), and I continued to be Brat (B for short).

Granny Brat passed away in 2000 after a long battle with cancer but almost until her death she was one of the dedicated and loving people who helped make SRD such a special home away from home.

—Amie Stone King
1993–1997

Letters from Home

The first semester I lived at SRD was fall 1964. I was a junior and had transferred from Kilgore Junior College. Move-in day was Sunday afternoon. My parents had driven me down on Saturday, and my father just insisted that we could move in on Saturday, if we would just show up and ask.

Mrs. McConnell, the headmistress of SRD, met my father that afternoon, and explained to him very patiently that Sunday afternoon was the ONLY time we could move in. He was really taken aback but acquiesced to her firmness.

That night we spent the night in the Driskill Hotel, and I cried myself to sleep at the newness of the experience.

My parents moved me in on Sunday afternoon, and Monday morning I had a letter from my mother in my mailbox. She had mailed it ahead of time so I would have a letter my first day at UT. She talked about the beautiful live oak trees out in front of the dorm and how I could draw strength from them. I was one forlorn young lady.

When they called me on the following Friday, my entire outlook had changed. I was thrilled and excited about being at UT.

Thirty-nine years later, I took my second son to Trinity University in San Antonio. We drove down on a Saturday and moved him in. We stayed for the family picnic out on the lawn of the beautiful campus. When it came time to depart, my son was one forlorn-looking young man. I had mailed him a letter so he could have mail on Monday.

When I called him three days later, he was thrilled and excited about being at Trinity. He had already settled in.

—JANE ARCHER FEINSTEIN
1964–1966, 1967

More Than Just "Housekeeping"

I've worked here for ten years and I really love my job. I'm a housekeeper.

There's a lot of things happening all the time. For instance, a couple of weeks ago around when school started, this lady from a room lost a friend in a car accident and they cried a lot. They were crying so much for their friend because that was a really sad thing for them to lose their friend.

I'm very fortunate because my girls are very neat. They are so good and neat and clean, maybe here and there I might have a nasty room, but for the most part, I just thank God all the time that these girls are so neat.

Amie: What's one of the best things about working here?

Everything's good. The pay's good, and we get a free meal. I just enjoy being around the young people, they are so good and so nice and friendly.

—MARY SANCHEZ, HOUSEKEEPER
1997–present

A Closing Thought

I'm Willie Pinson. I'm in the housekeeping department and it's a really great place to work. We have a lot of fun around here. I've worked here ten years.

A Good Friend

My friendship with ex-resident Leata Bartlett (formerly Brumby) began when she was a resident at SRD. Leata lived here in the mid to late '90s, and I really got to know her when she was an RA her senior year. We would often speak in passing, but our friendship really began after she moved away from the dorm.

It is a unique friendship, in that I am twelve years older than her, but we just seemed to "click." We had certain things in common, family values, morals, and interests. It was very much like an older/younger sister relationship.

When Leata got married in 2003, her family and friends all lived outside of Austin, so I helped her with many wedding things. I was the first one to see her in what she eventually chose as her wedding dress. She also included me in her wedding as an honorary bridesmaid. Since she married someone older, her husband, Rob, and my husband, Travis, are the same age. Needless to say, they hit it off, too.

After their marriage, they moved to Kyle, which is where we were living at the time. Unfortunately, we moved shortly afterward. We see each other as often as we can when our schedules permit. Leata still calls up to the dorm and asks me "What's for lunch?" and stops by periodically to see all of the staff. I have met many SRD girls since I have worked here, but none have resulted in a friendship like Leata's and mine. I know that she will be a friend for life.

—TRACY MUSSEY
Food Service Director, 1991–present

SRD Girls Concerned Over Illness of "Dad"

Protection for a house full of girls has been provided for

some 22 years by Edgar Lee "Dad" Walton, night watchman of Scottish Rite Dormitory, who has been admitted to Seton Hospital and is in critical condition.

"We have such a feeling of security when he's around," said Mrs. Lillian Jenks, bookkeeper. She remembers the panty raid last May, when Mr. Walton talked quietly and persuasively with the boys converging on the house.

The residents remember times he saved them from embarrassment by talking mildly to tipsy men until they were quiet and ready to leave or by catching peeping toms before even the girls were aware of their presence.

He was on call for anything at any time between 8:30 A.M. and 4:30 P.M.

Mr. Walton was born in Wise County February 6, 1893, and moved to Austin in 1928. He is the son of Mr. and Mrs. M.Y. Walton of Jonah. Mr. Walton has a wife, a daughter, two sisters, a brother, and a grandson.

Mr. Walton belongs to the Taylor Lodge of Masons and to the Shettles Memorial Methodist Church.

The grandson is his pride, "his hobby," Mrs. Cora Seymore, house counselor, said. The nine-month-old boy, Randy, has red hair and unfailing skill in getting along with his grandfather.

Mr. Walton is called "Dad" Walton by some of the girls living at SRD. He's gotten many a picture or Christmas gift from them, and in exchange he has often lent the girls nickels when they needed them for cold drinks and had no change. He has remarked that he has never lost a nickel—the girls always found him and paid.

The staff's opinion is that he "would be hard to replace . . ."

—PEGGY COCKRUM
The Daily Texan, October 28,
1952, reprinted with permission

UT Ex Ritter Returns for Austin Stockshow

Washing dishes at SRD and leading a parade down Congress Avenue Monday at 2 P.M. are on Tex Ritter's agenda when he returns to his old stomping grounds March 3–8 to perform in Austin's first annual Capital Area Stockshow.

The cowboy balladeer will appear at 8 P.M. each evening with White Flash, his horse in 70 Western pictures. Merle Travis, another guitar-playing hillbilly artist, will join Ritter, his guddy [sic] of California days.

Over 700 contestants from eleven Central Texas counties will participate in the daily livestock contests. Reserved seat tickets to see the stock and evening shows are $3.00, general admission is $1.80, and children's admission is 60 cents.

Way back in the late '20s the UT campus echoed nightly when Ritter in an enthusiastic quintet helped to elect Sam Johnson editor of the *Texan*. Ritter originally came to UT to study government and law. He earned part of his tuition washing dishes at SRD After he had been at the university five years, he kissed his law books goodbye and began the career which eventually landed him in New York and Hollywood. Since then he has had an outstanding career as radio, screen, and recording star.

—THE DAILY TEXAN
March 2, 1952
reprinted with permission

Tex Ritter was born Maurice Woodward Ritter in Murvaul, Texas, the son of James Everett Ritter and Martha Elizabeth Matthews.

He grew up on his family's farm in Panola County and attended school in Carthage and Beaumont. After graduating with honors, he entered the University of Texas at Austin.

Ritter, one of the early pioneers of country music, soon became interested in show business. He produced many albums and starred in a variety of "singing cowboy" films. He married actress Dorothy Fay and they had two sons, Thomas and the very well known actor John Ritter.

The Daily Dozen of a Sardine

As others think—
1. Sleeping.
2. Eating.
3. Powdering and painting.

4. Flirting.
5. Eating.
6. Flirting.
7. Powdering and painting.
8. Sleeping.
9. Flirting.
10. Sleeping.
11. Powdering and painting.
12. Eating.

As it really is—
1. Arise at 6 A.M.
2. Take cold shower and clean room.
3. Breakfast at 7:10.
4. Make classes from 8 to 1.
5. Lunch at 1:10.
6. Lab from 2 to 5.
7. Committee meetings.
8. Dinner.
9. Two hours at the library or attending lectures.
10. Study from 10 to 1.
11. From 1 to 4 working on *Annual Sardine.*
12. From 4 to 6, SLEEP (if your roommate doesn't snore too loud).

—THE ANNUAL SARDINE
Volume 2, #1, 1923

My Time as a Waiter

I started as a dishwasher. You had to start that way. Most guys wanted to get out there with the girls as soon as possible.

When you were carrying a tray and you started to slip, you weren't worried about your arms or elbows. You were most concerned about the china. They actually kept a running total on how much you dropped and then they charged you for it later.*

Girls at SRD were no different than anywhere else. When the year first started, you had about a week or two to coax the girls you wanted at your table. If they got comfortable at a table, they would run off any other girl who tried to sit there so you looked for girls you might like to date and tried to attract them to your table.

The waiter group was kind of like a fraternity. There was pride in being able to clear your table first, but I never won because Betty ate so slowly, and, yet, I married her. All the waiters would be standing around waiting on her to finish but that didn't hurry her at all.

The waiters used to play intramural sports, flag football, etc. Most were dating girls from SRD, and we'd go out on group dates. For football games we'd go down to Lake Austin, find a picnic table, listen to the game on the radio and just hang out. We were the closest of friends.

On November 22, 1963, Marina, one of the ladies who helped in the kitchen, came in saying, "The President's been shot!" Because she was kind of high strung, we made fun of her, but she was so insistent that someone went out to their car, turned on the radio, came back in and said, "It is true. He's been shot. He's been shot down." We all asked if he was all right. Classes were cancelled and then we all knew.

—ALAN CHALFONT
1961–1965

*Sheila Sorgee, one of SRD's alumni board members, mentioned that when she lived at the dorm, waiters who dropped the special china were required to pay for it. Alan confirmed that practice with his recollections.

A Family Affair

I had reservations at SRD, but Charles, my husband, and I ran off and got married. Since then my sister, my daughters, my granddaughter and two of my nieces have lived here.

—Molly Hull

I remember that we had a curfew until my second year but then they did away with that. SRD was one of the last places to have a curfew.

—MELANIE HULL WATSON
1979–1981

We had a curfew but the security guard would never tell on you, so it was no big deal. I remember one night I signed out with a sleeping bag and a pillow headed to the South Mall for a protest. They even had bed check at the dorm that night because so many girls had signed out with sleeping bags. Still, it didn't seem to matter where you were going as long as you had signed out.

—MELISSA HULL HENSHAW
1968–1973

Beauty Is a Pinch

In the fall of 1940 when we came for rush week, we wore wool since we were expected to dress in fashion. After an entire week of wearing wool in the blazing Texas September temperatures, I came home to SRD quite ill and was put in the infirmary for six days. Finally, on Friday I was allowed to come down from my room and was excited because the next day was the first football game of the season. It rained the entire game, we just sat there not thinking anything about it, but when we got back to SRD, Ms. Dehoney and all the other matrons* met us at the door. They all took turns fussing at my date while taking me back to the infirmary.

—MYRA LEE SUMMERS
1940–1942

*The dictionary definition of a matron is, a woman who supervises women and children, but at SRD matrons were usually somewhere between a grandmother and a warden.

A Rosy Reward

Every year after the Christmas Dinner there was entertainment in the living room. Anyone with a special talent was welcome and invited to participate. My roommate Kathryn and I both played the flute and performed numerous times at this annual event. Our freshman year we were asked to perform during the alumni reunion, and we quickly agreed. Everyone was very kind and appreciative, and both being performers at heart we were happy to have an audience. The next day we returned to our room after classes to find two vases each filled with a half dozen fresh roses from the SRD garden. We had no idea SRD had such a wonderful treasure hidden just down the hill. The roses were a great surprise and yet another reminder that SRD was a special place where we were loved and encouraged.

—Amie Stone King
1993–1997

A Heartfelt Memory

What sticks with me the most about SRD (and sometimes almost makes me cry) is how thankful I am for the wonderful friends I made there. I only lived there for one year and one summer, but in that relatively short time I came away with some wonderful friends that mean so much to me and I know I will have forever. Amie, Casey, and Jessica C. are as good, if not closer friends, than the friends I've had in Mount Pleasant since I was two years old. I truly loved Stella. Having lived my entire life in such a small town where everyone knew me, it was so reassuring to have Susie, Mary, and Stella all know me and feel like they truly cared about me. UT's a great school, but the main reason I feel so strongly about Emi (my daughter) going to UT is so she can live at SRD and feel loved and safe just like I did and make wonderful friends there that she will have her entire life.

—Meredith Cobb Joubert
1994–1995

Love and Support

I have many happy memories of my senior year at SRD, but one sad one to share. Mary did an excellent job of pairing my freshman roommate and me together. We both participated in similar activities in high school and even shared the same favorite color, purple. We were roommates for our first two years at SRD. She was diagnosed with cancer our junior year, and I didn't hear much from her that year other than she was hoping to return for our senior year.

The summer came and went, I received a birthday card from her, and my senior year began. One morning after my first class, Mary pulled me into her office and asked if I had heard the latest information. Her treatments had not been successful, and she was in hospice care. Nothing could have prepared me for that shock, but I was so grateful that Mary told me. It gave me the chance to let her family know how much my family and I cared about them. That weekend my mom and I made the trip to her hometown to visit her family at the hospice. It was truly one of the hardest things I have ever had to do.

In October of my senior year, she passed away. Even writing about it now, several years later, brings tears to my eyes. While her passing saddened me, I had an excellent group of friends to lean on. It was hard to lose a friend so young, but it made me realize how lucky I was to have such a wonderful support group there at SRD. My friends (and my parents) helped me get through it, and I will always be grateful for that.

—CARRIE NELSON
2000–2004

SRD Exhibits Paintings

Scottish Rite Dormitory boasts an art exhibit of eight paintings done by resident art majors of that dormitory. The display includes the paintings of Alice Combest, Sharon Lee Ellis, Sally Morris, Sharon Richey, and Charlotte Guzick.

The exhibit of landscapes, scenes from still-life, an abstract, and a portrait are displayed in the Scottish Rite Dormitory recreation room.

According to Mrs. Madie Morgan, a counselor at SRD, the art exhibit will be charged about once a month. Eight paintings will be chosen from those submitted by the residents of the dormitory to be displayed.

—THE DAILY TEXAN
December 17, 1963
reprinted with permission

Daddy Was a Mason

When we came down to look around at UT, Daddy said, "Let's go look at SRD," and I said, "You have to be the daughter of a Mason to live there," and he said, "Yes, I know. Let's go look." I think he was at UT when the dorm opened, and I had no idea he was a Mason. It was a good thing because I really enjoyed my time at SRD.

When I lived there, you were not allowed to have a car until you were a junior or had a certain amount of hours. My junior year I had a car so I could go do my elementary education observations. The freedom a car offered was fun since we could drive anywhere we wished.

One day I had a car full of girls and we were coming into the East parking lot and somehow I hit the tree, which stands in the middle of the divided driveway. I never confessed to my father how the car got that dent.

—Sylvia Hulsey West
1960–1964

Waiters and Friends

My first serious boyfriend was a waiter at SRD. His name was Gene Raborn. I have no idea whatever became of him. We met in the recreation room of SRD. Every Thursday night, my roommate Gay and I watched *The Fugitive* at 9 P.M. on the television downstairs. One night three waiters came in for some reason. Grover McMains spotted my roommate Gay and went for her like a bee to a flower. I talked to a second waiter (Gene). Later, both young men called us, and we began dating. Oh, my. There is nothing like a first college romance.

Gene graduated one year before I did, went to work for Brown and Root in Silsbee, Texas, and ended our romance. I was left forlorn again. He later went to Kuwait and then I don't know. He has disappeared so well that even Google can't resurrect him!

Grover was in the Air Force ROTC, became a pilot, married, and had at least one son, Merrick. I ran into Grover at an ice cream place in Austin about 1984 or so, but I haven't seen him since. Our other waiter friends were Turner Bratton and Abner Kestler. Abner was from Hooks, Texas, and was kin to Ben Barnes. Turner and Abner were ambulance drivers and picked up a number of people that Whitman shot at the tower. Grover and Abner were managers of the Rio Grande Apartments and rented Gay and me an apartment the weekend of the shooting.

Jeffrey Wentworth was another waiter. He was in law school at the time he waited tables at SRD. Later I ran into him when I was teaching at Texas Tech. Funny how it truly is a small world especially when it comes to SRD.

—Jane Archer Feinstein
1964–1966, 1967

A Family Tree

We have a unique SRD thread running through our family. My late mother-in-law, Shelby Zempter Eanes Mowat, lived in the dorm in the late 1920s and/or early '30s and in 1931 married Robert Hill Eanes of Austin, a direct descendent of the Robert Eanes of Austin for whom the elementary school and school district are named.

I, Laura Becker Eanes, lived in SRD 1951–'53 (rooms 19 and 21) and in 1958 married their son Robert Zempter Eanes of Galveston.

In 1989 our son Robert Becker Eanes of Atlanta, Georgia, married Clare Poerschke, who lived in SRD from 1983–'85.

Their son (our grandson) Robert Hill Eanes II was born in 1998, and we are wondering if this Eanes–SRD connection will continue in the future for a fourth generation!

—Laura B. Eanes
1951–1953

A Conversation with Stella

What are some things that you have seen or experienced as either a housekeeper or resident director that have made you laugh or cry? What are your memorable stories about being part of this place?

Well memorable is when I see all the girls that I've gotten to know, come back to visit with their families.

Experiences? There's a lot, you know, it's just like raising kids over and over and over.

I've really enjoyed working here.

I worked in housekeeping for 25 years and when I was offered the job of RD I was thrilled because I thought to myself, "I'll be here all the time with the girls," and my immediate family was happy, too, that I could stay here.

Experiences like chasing boys out of the halls. Finding out things . . . I know girls do sneaky things but . . . it's just been a lot of fun.

I feel sad when the girls get sick, and I try my best and try to comfort them and get them to talk to their moms. I've really enjoyed it and it's gonna be sad when I leave.

Are you planning to leave anytime soon?

No, no, no, no, not really, but you can't stay forever.

I know you have to have stories, specific stories.

Letting them in and have them tell me stories that I didn't want to hear but I heard it, things they've done and are ashamed of. When they've been drinking they just tell you all the bad things they do.

So you've taken confession?

Yes, I tell them, "It's okay, honey, you don't have to tell me and they say, 'But I want to.'" "Okay, well, tell me."

There was this girl not too long ago who went to a Tiki party and had an argument with her boyfriend, and she felt bad because she still loved him. "But I did this terrible thing" she said, and I said, "What did you do?" and she said "But I can't tell you because you wouldn't like me anymore."

I'm like, "Oh no, I would still like you," but she just couldn't tell me.

It's just girls having a good time, coming home crying, breaking up with their boyfriends. It's like raising my 17-year-old granddaughter.

My 20-year-old grandson used to come here when he was five years old; he's at SFA now.

What do you think of the waiters?

I've managed to meet a lot of the waiters. They are wonderful, and of course, you know that, Amie.

They'll ask me, "Stella, do you know any nice girls"? "They're all nice," I'll say.

He sorta likes so and so. "Do you know if she has a boyfriend." Same thing goes for the girls who like some of the waiters. "Stella, I like that guy, he's so cute. Do you know his name? Does he have a girlfriend?" I don't know, it's fun stuff like that, and I'll go and I'll investigate, and I'll find out he does have a girlfriend, and I feel bad going back to the girl and telling her he does have a girlfriend, but I tell her you never know. They might break up.

I just enjoy so many things about SRD. When I worked in housekeeping, I used to do my job and go home. Living here is wonderful, I just love it here.

How do you deal with girls at 3:00 A.M.?

It's pretty scary when I see them like I see them, but God helps me. I stay with them until their roommate gets home. I'll spend the night on the floor sometimes until the roommates get there. They're very thankful in the morning. It's very scary to see the girls drink so much when they don't know what they are doing. I've had to call EMS a couple of times.

Suzie has been great, been wonderful. She's the one who hired me. She says, "Stella I don't know how you can do this."

The girls expect a lot.

I'm kind of like their grandmother. They're really so respectful, sometimes more than my own grandkids.

I always just tell them I'm doing this for your own good, and if you've been drinking, stay in bed, and don't get up and hurt yourself.

Were you here when the girl crawled out on the balcony?

No, I was out of town. I was off that weekend,

When I got back, Perla said, "How could you leave me?"

It was her first time to have something major like that happen.

Any particular men you remember escorting off the hall?

Well you know, Amie, there have been so many, and I know the girls are nice, and I love them all, but they do lie.

One time walking the halls I heard a man's voice, and it was almost midnight, and I was like okay they know when visiting hours are over. I knew where the voice was coming from, so I knocked and knocked and I said, "I'm sorry but you know boys are not supposed to be up here now."

"Oh, there's no boy in here."

So I said "Okay," because we are not allowed to go into the rooms and search. She closed the door, but I still stayed in the hallway and I had my radio, and I heard the voice again, and I was like, "Come on, I know he's planning to spend the night in there." I did like I turned my radio on, but I really didn't, and I stood right in front of the door and talked into the walkie-talkie and I said, "Maintenance, I need your help up here. There's a guy, and he won't leave. Could you help me, and can you bring you know what?" That's all I said.

I don't know why I said that, it just came to me. And then it was amazing, two doors down the hall of 3rd Central flew open and two guys came out. I did talk loud on the radio. Then the boy that the girl said wasn't in there, he looked at me and ran down the stairs. He was lucky because if it had been past midnight he'd have been locked in. I don't know why I said, "Bring you know what." They probably were wondering what are they going to bring, but it worked! I got three guys out and it was so funny I just started laughing when I got back to my room!

You see, Marillah, don't hide any boys when you come to college because I will find them. (*Marillah is my 4½ year old daughter.*)

The girls expect me to do my walk at the same time every night, but I try and change, and I've caught girls drinking.

One time I was walking behind two girls, and I knew they were really out of it, and they turned around and saw me and one girl told the other one, "Don't look back. The Warden is behind us."

You know, there was another house mom before Miss Pennington and when the girls were really bad and would wake her up early in the morning, the next morning she would get up with an iron skillet and a spoon and wake them up at 6:00 by standing in front of their doors beating on it and saying, "Good morning, it's 6:00 A.M.!" Her name was Ms. Harrington. I used to clean her suite, and she would tell me, "Thank goodness for Mexican dresses because when they wake you up in the middle of the night you can just throw it on and go."

How did you come to work here?

Actually I went to the employment office. I needed a job desperately

Were you a single mom?

Yes, I was raising my son and daughter. And I had just been laid off from my other job, and I went to the employment office, and they told me they needed a housekeeper at Scottish Rite Dormitory. So I came and applied, and the housekeeper at that time was Ms. Johnson. She said, "Can you start Monday? " And I was like, "Oh, my God. Really!" Because I needed a job desperately. We talked, and she liked my information. I've been here ever since.

When Suzie offered me the job as RD, my son Mark said, "Mom are you sure you want to take this job? Do you really want to live there?" I said I could try it and see so I asked Suzie, "If this doesn't work out, could I have my housekeeping job back?" She didn't give me a yes or no.

I've just enjoyed living here I love it, and I hope to survive and stay another few years!

—Stella Reyes
Housekeeping for 25 years
Resident Director, 1997–present

More Than Just Waiters

Since I began working at SRD in 1991, sixteen years ago, I have seen many guys come and go. Each one is a little different than the last. Being in my mid-twenties when I began made me really close to the same age as some of the senior waiters. So, at that time, I was not only their supervisor, but like a big sis to many of them. I have heard many a story, most of which I shouldn't repeat . . . so I won't. I can say that I have hired a bunch, fired a few and watched many grow into the young men that they are today.

I have been invited to many a party, of which I can honestly say, I have not been able to make. I have seen many of them get their hearts broken; yet several have found their soul mates (some of which were SRD girls). I have been invited to several weddings, some of which I was lucky enough to attend.

Numerous guys have gone on to travel around the world. Just to name a few . . . one started out in Haiti, working for the Peace Corps. Then traveled to Japan and Spain, teaching English in both places. This particular man landed back in Japan with a job and got married there this year (this one I couldn't attend).

Another success story was a quiet little freshman who worked here all the way through school and then traveled around the world for a couple of years. He now works for NASA and trained the latest crew that launched this past month.

Yet another is working for the Boston Red Sox organization. He also married an SRD ex-RA, and they have a baby now. Some have gone on to graduate programs and received masters degrees. Some have become doctors, lawyers, engineers, teachers, and so on. Many of them still keep in touch and occasionally stop by the dorm. Since I do not have any children of my own yet, I attribute part of that to the fact that I have already been blessed with "raising" my own boys here at SRD. I can only say that there is never a dull moment and that they have kept me young at heart over the years.

—TRACY MUSSEY
Food Service Director
1991–present

SRD Nips Hargrove by One Penetration

In a game marked by tight defenses and a high wind from the north, the SRD Dark Horses defeated a tough Hargrove Hustlers team on penetrations, 1-0, after the Class A intramural touch football feature ended in a scoreless tie Thursday.

Faced with the realization of the game being neither a victory nor loss, the Dark Horses penetrated for the first time with ten seconds left to play. Thus the winners advanced further into Class A Independent play along with Amery who whipped Barebacks, 25-6.

[And later] SRD's Dark Horses took the measure of Amery on penetrations, 3-2 after the game had closed with a 6-6 tie.

—EDDIE HUGHES
Excerpts, The Daily Texan
reprinted with permission

A Darkhorse Tale

In 1941 after I finished junior college in Tyler, Texas, I was planning to continue my education and since all my friends were going to Texas A&M, I went down there first but could not find a job.

I came to UT and found that pickings were pretty slim but was able to apply at SRD. Mrs. Stripe was the business manager at the time, and she told me her crew was already set and that there was very little turnover because people tended to keep their jobs all four years.

I returned to Tyler, and about five days before the semester started she called and told me she had a job for me in the scullery. If it hadn't been for that job, I couldn't have come to college because neither my folks nor I had any money.

At the time I was 20 about to be 21 in December, and the war started in December, which makes me think I probably would have been drafted in a heartbeat. I like to say that SRD saved my life. It's always been like a shrine to me, and I have really deep feelings for the place. What a pleasure to be here.

—JAMES R. HUTTON
1941–1943

"Darkhorses" is the name given to a group of waiters from the early years of the dorm who have regular social gatherings and meet every other year at SRD.

Yes, Marillah, Daddy Was a Waiter

SRD had a long tradition of seated meals. The bell rang at a certain time, girls lined up outside the dining room doors,

proceeded to the tables and were served family style by waiters. When I lived there, the waiters at SRD were college men
and usually frat boys. Many of them were very cute and most
were friendly and indulgent. One night our table persuaded a
waiter named John to make sure all of our desserts were the
same size. He did it with a smile.

After 1993 there were no longer seated lunches, only
seated dinners, and Sunday lunch, to which wearing a dress
was required. Too bad the code didn't say anything about hair
and makeup because I saw plenty of wrinkled dresses and
sleepy faces at that meal. It was no longer the proper, pious
experience it once had been. During this time, changes were
happening all over the dorm and by the next year there were
no seated dinners.

Although there was a lot of complaining about having to be
at dinner at 6:00 P.M., it was actually a wonderful time to visit
with friends and decompress from the day. I was a theatre
major and had to work long hours in the costume shop, but
the shop staff understood SRD's rules and would let me leave
for dinner and return later.

My then future husband Matt joined the waiter force in the
fall of 1995. He was not a new face since I'd met him pre-
viously at parties. But suddenly he was a very attractive
face, and I made it a goal to befriend him. After about five
months, we started dating. For our first date he called me
from the SRD house phone in the lobby right after his shift to
see if I wanted to go out later that evening. We went to a
movie and on to Kerby Lane Café for coffee. He had forgotten
to stop by the ATM on his way to pick me up, so I paid for the
date. As a joke, his brother reimbursed me the $10 at our
wedding.

We dated for a year, and on the night we were engaged, he
planned a surprise Easter egg treasure hunt for me. The RA at
the front desk was in on the whole thing and listened as I
ranted and raved about an egg treasure hunt. I wanted to go
out with Matt, not hunt eggs with a group.

Matt managed to drag me over to the Tower where he had
hidden several eggs, and we were engaged on the steps of the
east side of the tower. Yes, I was one of the "Waiter Daters,"
and I know I got one of the best.

Today we live near Austin. When our daughter was born, the dorm administrator laughed and said she was their first SRD baby. Now she is four and very much an SRD girl in training.

—AMIE STONE KING
1993–1997

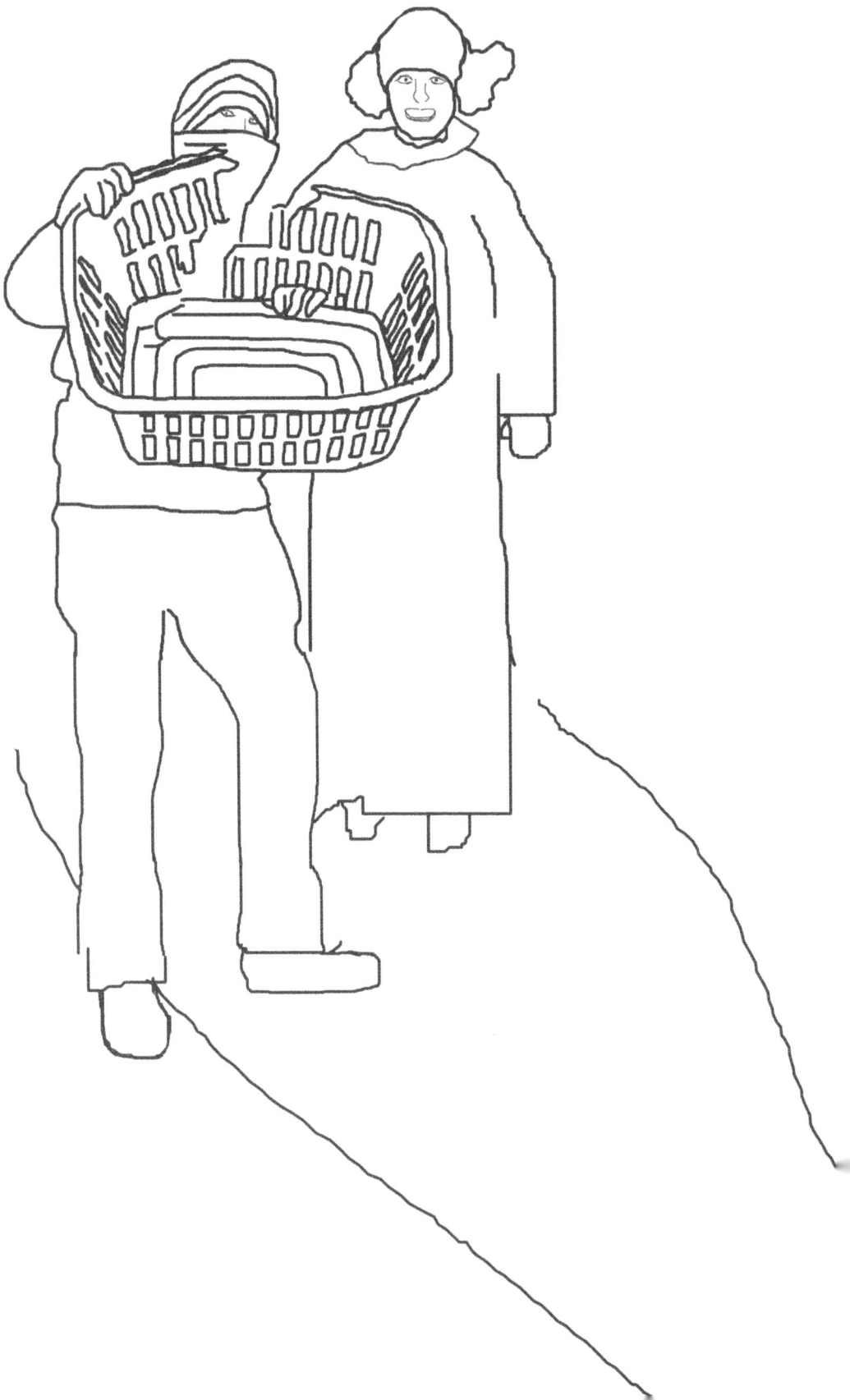

How Far Will They Bend?

The Stash

I started as the Registrar of SRD July 5, 1994. I loved the environment and working with the college students. I went to college down the road at SWTSU (now Texas State). My friends and I would come to Austin to "socialize" and I laugh as I recall that as long as we could see the UT tower, we were able to make our way back to IH 35 and home to San Marcos.

In 1977 I was a sophomore in college. I was an RA (Resident Assistant) at Falls Hall, and being the enterprising group that we were, decided we wanted staff T-shirts. We did a car wash before the start of classes and earned enough money to cover the cost of the shirts. Now back in the day (as my children would say), one of the more popular brands of beers was Falstaff. We could not think of a better logo for our shirt than to borrow an idea from the beer company. So printed on the front of our shirts was the beer logo and instead of the real name of the beverage it was "Falls Staff."

Back to the summer of 1994. During the regular summer maintenance work I was walking the halls trying to get a feel for the grand old building. SRD has always had the rule of no alcohol in the building, but on that day while walking the hall, I saw a familiar looking site. There were at least 12 Falstaff beer bottles standing in line down the middle of the hall.

The maintenance men said they were working on the ceiling, and when they went to move one of the ceiling tiles, one of the bottles dropped down. After further investigation, they pulled down the old discarded bottles. (I did some research and Falstaff stopped production in the early 1980s.)

Our best guess is that some of the residents were having a party and needed to get rid of the evidence. Stashing it in the ceiling would ensure that the housekeeping staff would not find it in their rooms and turn them in to the administration. I took one of the bottles and put it in my office as a memento of my college years and a reminder that some things never change.

A few years later, I was helping a father of a prospective resident in my office. I've collected memorabilia over the years and have it displayed in my office. One of the pieces that I have displayed is my Falstaff beer bottle. This father happened to notice the bottle and seemed very displeased that I had it displayed. I tried to explain the significance it held for me and assured him that it was not SRD's policy to allow drinking in the dorm. I can't remember if his daughter ever lived at SRD, but again, some things never change.

Parents send their daughters to UT and SRD hoping for a good education and protected living environment. Daughters go to UT and live at SRD hoping for a good education and excitement about their newfound freedom.

—MARY MAZUREK
Registrar, 1994–present

The Complete Guide to Perfect Ladyhood
(Handbook for SRD Girls)

Soon as the first bell rings in the early dawn, it is well for the cleanly maiden to arise and grab herself a tub, lest in waiting until the second bell she lose her chance. Woe be unto the sluggard who shall arise with the third bell and hope for a place where within to lave her person!

Cribbing one's roommate's last clean towel is the second great law for health, for without a towel the cleanly maiden shall surely catch cold.

Of the two evils, being late to breakfast is far less than not arriving at all, for Shakespeare has said: "Better late than never," and "A bird in the hand gathers no moss."

To masticate one's orange without having first squirted it into the eyes of all who behold is the grossest of poor morals.

Trying to cut one's bacon is useless. Therefore the wise maiden will seize it manfully in both hands and thus conquer it.

If the attempt to omit those articles of clothing vulgarly called hose is successful, it is well worth the trouble; for surely comfort comes before the eyesight of those who have never seen legs.

Scan *The Daily Texan* with diligence every morning, for this is the mark of real collegiate breeding.

Hasten with all speed to that 8 o'clock, but never let haste govern thy body to the detriment of thy soul—in other words, if it is necessary to cut, do so.

Realize thy limitations and do not strive to prepare for every class every day. Once in two weeks is ample.

In the rush of thy daily duties do not fail to seek recreation and Cokes at every possible moment. Health and peace of mind are of greater importance than the demands of one's professor.

Trotting home for the mail at 10:30 every morning is the main aim in the life of the upright maiden.

Even when there is no mail for thee, smile bravely, for mayhaps thou wilt catch a ride back to the campus.

—MARY NUNN
The Annual Sardine, May 1926

Curfew

I lived on the fourth floor of SRD, as a freshman, in 1970. There were about 30 of us.

I was enrolled in Plan II and had Irwin Spear for biology. All I did was study biology, for Irwin Spear. I rarely left the fifth floor study hall.

In 1970, as freshmen, we were not allowed to stay out past the midnight curfew during our first semester at SRD. If our parents gave permission, however, we could have "hours" during our second semester and bypass curfew.

So in the spring of 1971 my parents gave me permission to stay out after midnight. Little good it did me as I was always studying for Plan II.

One day a very good friend of mine that I'll call Mary, who lived on the second floor, asked if she could "borrow" my name to sign out and sign back in, as her parents had not given her permission to stay out late. "Why not?" I said. And so she did.

The months passed, and at long last my first year at UT ended. I had finished all my finals. It was a lovely evening in late May. I decided to go out and celebrate with friends. I, of course, did not get back to the dorm until around 2:00 A.M.

I approached the guard and signed in as Amy Marable. He looked at me for awhile then said, "Young lady, you are not Amy Marable."

"Yes sir, I am!" I said.

"I know Amy Marable," he said, "and she has blond hair, not brown like yours, and is about four inches taller."

I realized immediately, of course, that my friend Mary had signed out on my name more than once during that spring of 1971! Rather than get us both in a great deal of trouble, I admitted to the guard that he was "right," and I walked away.

I slept in the trees behind the dorm that night. When the doors opened the next morning, I resumed my identity as Amy Marable.

If there is a moral to this story it is lost on me. I have just kept this as one of many wonderful memories of my incredible days at Scottish Rite Dorm and UT, minus Irwin Spear and biology, of course.

—AMY MARABLE MCBRIDE
1970–1971

Ice Storm

A friend of mine lived on the south side of the 4th floor at SRD, and one day she and her roommate decided it would be fun to go out on the balustrade and throw ice down onto the passing waiters as they walked in front of SRD.

This quickly sparked a desire for retaliation, and someone told the matron who stormed upstairs and quickly counted doors and windows as she walked down the hall in an effort to find the culprits. At this point my friend and her roommate were scrambling into their room and closing the window as fast as they could. Soon there was a knock on the door next to them, and the matron burst in demanding to know who had been throwing ice. The bewildered girls in the next room honestly told her they had no idea.

Due to a miscalculation on the matron's part she had chosen the wrong door. If she had been correct in her counting, my friend and her roommate would have been in deep trouble because even if they had tried to deny it, there were muddy footprints all over the carpet!

—BECKY SHANNON EADDY
1973-1975

Laundry Cart Thrill Ride

A friend and I had always wanted to ride in one of the laundry carts that the dorm employees used to transport the linens.

I don't know if they are still in use, but they were rectangle shaped and made of heavy canvas, about three feet tall, on four rollers.

After a few days of experimental riding in the carts, I decided my friend should go for a really good ride. She got inside and I pushed the cart over to the ramp that runs from the laundry room down to the dining hall.

It was immediately apparent this might have been a bad idea. She went really fast and crashed into the closed glass dining room doors. It is a miracle that the glass didn't break and she wasn't hurt.

After we calmed down, it was pretty funny, but that event cured us from wanting to ride in the laundry carts ever again.

—ANONYMOUS
1972–1975

In and Out

Well, it had to have been 1959–1960. I was in school in San Marcos (SWT/TSU) and my friend Rita was at UT and living in SRD. We were planning her upcoming wedding, and I was in Austin for the weekend.

She planned for me to spend the night in SRD. Now, you have to understand, Rita is as close to perfect as you can get and this infraction of SRD rules still amazes me! She gave me my explicit instructions on how we were going to "pull this off." Ha! I didn't even make it up the stairs.

I was caught and escorted out the doors (as well as I can remember). I had no alternative plan until I thought of friends living on campus. So, off I went on foot until I reached their dorm and begged for lodging. (This part I remember very well!)

—JACKIE THORNTON
SRD Friend

Smooching

Some of the young people don't realize that we have cameras all over the property. They like to hang out in the hammocks and canoodle and make out, and the maintenance men watch them for a minute or two and then walk over and explain they are on live TV.

A current resident in the office interjected that there was a place where the cameras couldn't see you in the backyard/ hammock area.

—TERRY SHEARER
Resident Director,
2006-2007

The Sewing Project

When I lived at SRD, the big room on the top floor was a study hall. One semester in home economics we had a project in sewing. I was never quite the outstanding student because I was too much of a people person. For this assignment I was making a Kelly green wool jacket with white piping and big bone buttons. I was behind and never was much of a seamstress.

My grandmother was a good seamstress, and she taught me how to do things *quickly*, and they wanted me to do it *properly*, which was a problem. Thankfully, we could take our work home.

Still, at SRD the lights went out at 11 P.M. For a week, I

snuck down to the ironing room, turned on the light and tried to finish putting the lining in my jacket. I swore I would never make another one, and I haven't!

—JERRY COCHRAN MOORE
1944–1945

Jerry and her friend Helen were SRD roommates who married Joe Moore and Jim Roddy, respectively, and remain friends even today.

The Physics Lesson

Bored from an early semester ice storm that held us hostage in the dorm, my friend and I decided to salvage the day by sledding down the steep driveway to the lower parking lot. Searching for the perfect sled we decided on two green laundry baskets.

After a few minutes on the gently sloping parking lot hill, we decided that was not offering enough thrill so we went over to investigate the walkway that led from the lower lot to the upper level. At one point the walk is at about a 50 degree angle (or so it seems when you're trying to hike up it on a hot summer day), with a sharp turn about half-way down.

We calculated the risks for a few minutes, created a plan of action and decided to give it a try. Our baskets fit side-by-side on the track, which was perfect, we thought, as we could "help" each other if things got out of control.

About a millisecond after shoving off, it was apparent that things were indeed out of control, and there was nothing we could do about it. Somehow my basket passed in front of hers, and I went under the railing, whacking my hand on the iron post and crashing into the ivy on the other side of the path. She managed to make it further down before landing in the groundcover.

This should have been a sign that enough was enough, but being the daredevil that she was, she hopped up and said she was giving it another try. Again we thought, calculated, and devised a plan for her next attempt.

The idea was for me to stand near the post where she had left the track the first time, reach out and push her so she would continue to stay on the path and then we'd see how far she'd make it. We failed to consider the laws of physics, especially the one about "a body in motion tends to stay in motion" and, in this case, on the same trajectory.

She was ready at the top of the hill, and I was standing in the ivy ready to push her out of harm's way. What happened next took literally about three seconds. She came flying at me, I did my best to push her, her ankle slammed into the iron post, the basket crashed into the post, I fell backwards, and she landed sprawled in the flower bed next to me. Did I mention the loud "pop" as her leg hit the post? She broke her leg right above the ankle and had a huge gash in her shin where the bone was visible.

She refused to let me take her to the hospital because of the icy streets, and she sat for a day with her broken leg wrapped in an ankle splint.

The next day when we finally braved the icy conditions and went to the emergency room, the doctor laughed at us and asked if we had been "totally smashed" at the time. We sweetly told him we were actually completely sober. It was almost too much for him to believe.

Perhaps physics should be a required class for all UT students because we certainly didn't grasp the concepts!
—AMIE STONE KING
1993–1997

Our friend Meredith, after hearing our story, admitted to having rollerbladed down the ramp. It wasn't as fun as she thought it would be either.

Juanita

During my first year at SRD, I lived on the 3rd floor with my roommate and friend from high school, Sandi Spaid Shomber. Being an animal lover, I can't exactly recall how it happened; I came home to SRD with a gerbil. We harbored our pet and affectionately decided to name her Juanita, after the dorm mother. The gerbil, unfortunately, escaped and chewed a hole in the dress of a gal who was none too pleased. (I later reimbursed her for damages.)

When Juanita got out of her cage, we could always tell where she was by the shrill screams in the hall.

The real Juanita of course discovered our stowaway and after my confession, insisted we release the animal immediately. She escorted me to the parking lot, and I struggled as we let Juanita loose, not to wave goodbye and call her by name!

—ALLISON EDWARDS
1983–1985

A Special Place

SRD was a different world, even then. Like other dorms, SRD was all female, locked its doors at a certain time each night and restricted male access even during the daytime. But no other dorm had that magnificent, opulent living room that stretched almost the full length of the first floor. There sometimes, my roommate Margaret entertained us all at the grand piano. And on weekends visiting family members gathered in small groups. At the end of a day of classes, walking up through the tree-shaded yard and through the grand living room made it natural to walk with a special confidence.

In the decade of free love, when the contraceptive pill was new, we were gathered together in the assembly room for the annual lecture, "The Best Contraceptive Is the Verbal No." Curfews were amazingly early and very real. Decorum was encouraged.

We ironed our clothes in the "smokers" at the end of each hallway—rooms set aside long before our time so that the girls would not sit on the front walk to smoke but come inside, out of sight, instead. No one could come to breakfast in pajamas. We wore instead ugly ill-fitting shifts. At other meals, skirts were thrown over shorts—but at Sunday dinner no one wanted to miss the vanilla ice cream rolled in crushed Oreo cookie.

SRD was a normal world, yes, then. The front doors were locked, but there were always fire escapes for the more daring. And most everyone needed a late night pizza delivery. Forbidden whiskey lived in a crevice in the top of many a closet doorframe. The aging building struggled with a burgeoning variety of electric appliances.

Friendships flourished; many would last a lifetime. And a special bond was born between each of us and all the others from other times who had lived at SRD. For a time it was home. Forever it is a special place.

—JANICE GREGORY
1964–1967

Lost in Space

My friend committed grand larceny at SRD but eventually made good. When I worked here, there were framed moon shots hanging on the walls in the Rec Room. One day, for fun, my acquaintance stole them. His SRD girlfriend at the time took them off the walls and handed them to him through the Rec Room windows.

It was supposed to be a joke, and he was planning to return them, but instead decided to wrap them all and give them to the other waiters as Christmas gifts. When I opened mine, I was like, "What am I supposed to do with this? I can't return it!"

Finally, my graduation came and I left the photograph with my roommates and told them I was washing my hands of the matter. One of them was a nervous fellow, and he decided to return the picture because no one knew him. He walked into SRD and said, "Here, I want to return this," and tried to go, but the RA on duty grabbed him and would not let him leave.

Needless to say he spilled the beans and named names and then told me what he'd done. I called my friend and said, "You have to do something about this." He didn't have any good ideas and said he wasn't going to take care of it so I told him, "When they come to me, I'm sending them to you." This spurred him on. He collected them all and then handed them back to his girlfriend through the Rec Room windows where she re-hung them on the walls.

—SHANNON PHILLIPS
Waiter, 1980–1982

The "Pit"

One of my dearest friends and I lived in the "Pit"—too many good stories come from the Pit. At an anniversary celebration my friend and I attended when the Pit was "maids' quarters," young women looked at us with wide glaring eyes as if we were dinosaurs and exclaimed, "YOU LIVED in the PIT!!!" As if human inhabitants there were unheard of, which was really funny to us.

My friend and I (Suzy Morton Toelkes) lived in the largest single rooms in the whole dorm across the hall from each other in the Pit. Someone told me that because the window slats in the Pit were constantly being removed to avoid curfew that they decided to no longer use the area for rooms. Can't imagine?

—ALLISON EDWARDS
1983–1985

The UT Column

Girls living in Scottish Rite Dormitory are allowed to have but a very few electric appliances in their rooms. They might have say, a radio and electric alarm clock.

One of SRD's brightest smuggled in an electric popcorn popper recently and hid it. She kept the Wesson oil in a shampoo bottle.

The inevitable happened one night. Quite excited about being asked out, she rushed in late in the afternoon, grabbed the wrong bottle and gave her scalp one of those real oil treatments.

—CHARLIE SMITH
The Daily Texan, May 7, 1961
reprinted with permission

Prim and Proper?

The craziest thing I remember happening at SRD is when the girls down the hall hired a male stripper for another girl's birthday, and he actually stripped in the girl's room. So much for no men above the ground floor! (This is actually a different occurrence from the 1994 stripper.)

Another time when we had not had CCB's all year, the girls decided a protest was in order. They "wrapped" the parlor in toilet paper on which was written over and over, "We want CCB's!" They got in huge trouble, but I seem to remember that we also got CCB's.

—CHRISTY PETERS WATSON
1991–1993

Man on the Hall

Actually, it was May 1994. I remember because I believe it was Valerie's birthday in May. Maybe it was the giddiness of too many late nights studying, or perhaps a carb high from Double-Dave's pepperoni rolls, but somehow with finals approaching, several girls on the floor decided it would be too much fun to hire a stripper and sneak him in for a birthday surprise.

Please know that I was normally the ever-responsible RA and this event was not at all reflective of our hall's normal activities. (We just won't mention the one-time training session by one hall resident on how to do Tequila shots and the late night scavenging of the Fiji's outdoor holiday decorations to procure an evergreen branch "tree" for the holiday decorating contest. Our hall certainly smelled the most like Christmas!)

But back to the real story . . . Leslie and another of our intrepid residents put the first few semesters of their college education to work and went straight to the yellow pages to secure the appropriate resource in our price range (read: cheap).

Initially, I simply agreed to look the other way. But somehow—perhaps drawn in by the allure of being a good girl gone bad—I agreed to help sneak the guy in. Our cover story, if caught, was that he was someone's brother with permission to help move out.

In hindsight, how anyone would ever have believed that a guy in his mid-30s with long permy hair, wearing boots and tear away jeans with fringe (yes, fringe) on the side, being stealthily escorted up the back stairs while carrying a personal boom box, was any SRD resident's brother . . . well, let's just say we were hoping we wouldn't get caught.

I don't think most of us had ever seen a stripper before, but I can assure you that after this experience we were cured for life. The music, except that it was cheesy, was not memorable. He basically headed back to the sun room in question, popped his boom box on the dresser, and went to work.

I will leave the details to your imagination, but will make one comment—cellulite. Who knew guys could have it? And that we would ever be close enough to see it if they did? Like I said, cured for life. I think we all learned a valuable lesson that day. Bargains aren't always the best deal!

—Sabra Phillips
1992–1994, 1996–1997

"Main-*Tain!*-Ance Men"

I remember this one Maintenance Man that would shout out as he walked down the halls "Main–*Tain!*–Ance–Man." It was four distinct syllables with the accent on "Tain." To this day I still say maintenance man that way.

My room, 363, was on the NE corner by the fire escape. Mr. Giles, with the maintenance staff, showed me how to unhook the fire alarm if I ever wanted to use the fire escape. I never used it but had the option.

Also, there was a maintenance man who was young, cute, and knew it. His name was Mo. One night Mo was found in a resident's room and there was no forced entry.

When my parents would go to Dallas they would send me Almond Pecan Corn. It got to where the staff knew what was in the box by the size and address. So when I would get the

Almond Pecan Corn I would open it downstairs and take it to the "ladies": Mrs. Townes, Mrs. Evans, Mrs. Pruitt, Mrs. Potts. And also to most of the maintenance staff, cleaning staff, and kitchen staff. That paid off because when I had problems with my AC/heater I never had to wait for the maintenance crew.

—KATHY KEILS
1976–1980

What the Maintenance Man Saw

I'm here with Brian and Robert who are both maintenance men at SRD. Tommy is wandering in and out as we talk. Brian started here my senior year and Robert was already working in the kitchen when I came. What follows are the conversations we had about their time here at SRD.

On Rescuing the Girls . . .

I had to go get one girl on 26th Street. I don't know which building it was. She was parked on the side of the road. I had to change her tire on the side of the road there.

One girl needed her tire changed and she said, "Can you kind of teach me how to do it?" I replied, "Just a question, but didn't your dad ever teach you how to do it?" "Oh no," she said, "Our butler always did that."

I had to go get one girl who ran out of gas on 28th Street and get her going again.

Lots of battery starts.

Tommy's fixed a lot of cars around here!

(Tommy is now head of maintenance. At one point in his SRD career, he also owned a car repair service.)

Tommy claims not to remember anything but he once had to come to pick me up in the bus lane on the Drag after my transmission failed. My friend and I drove his Bronco back while he followed us driving in first gear; the only other gear the car would go into was reverse.

Brian asks me, "Did you live here when Donny got knocked out?" He saw some guys around the corner somewhere, and they jumped out from behind the bush and whap. He thinks they hit him with a pipe.

There was one night when I was working 11-7 and me and Perla was on duty, and a guy pulls up in a truck. He asked me to get some girls out of the truck, but I said I could help only if the guy would bring them on the SRD property. Then I could take them in the building. I called Perla and she helped bring them up.

Got them to their room and when she left, the two girls started arguing. When I got there one was laying in front of the AC, and the other one had gone out the window onto the 4th floor balcony. She was drunk and was trying to get back to her boyfriend. I managed to grab her and pull her back in to safety.

Now I've managed to corner Donny, another long time SRD maintenance man, in the maintenance office.

Here is his take on being hit by a man in the parking lot one night.

Lucky when it happened, when I did rounds I hid my keys. That time was crazy around here. Two–three o'clock in the morning. You girls didn't see the stuff around then. Yes, I got waylaid as you say.

All we had then in the East lot was the bonnet lights. Now we have a full "security" system complete with better lights, cameras, and a PA system.

There used to be, you know, we had some "wild" girls. I knew one girl, and she used to call me and say there was commotion going on. She lived right over Judge Hightower's office, and she'd call and say there was a fight (we worked alone at night then). I'd run over there to see what was going on, and while I was gone she'd let her boyfriend in with the keys.

There was some crazy events like one night I walked over and a girl said boys were bothering her, and there were two drunk guys and they caused a little trouble but there never a lot of trouble. Mainly it was boys trying to sneak in that kept me the busiest.

Sneaking in?

Do boys get in? I'm not going to lie, yes. They're sneaky, yeah, ya'll are.

Somebody in a pickup truck would pull next to the door and get where you couldn't see the door, and the girls would get out and walk around and open the door and the guys would stay down low and sneak in.

I chased my share through the hallways. I did take it serious, and it did bother me when somebody got in because I felt like I had failed.

We had one when I first started. I was working with Tommy. A guy got in on us somehow. We'd been told there was a guy coming out of the girls' bathroom. So we go up there and couldn't find him and the girls weren't sure where he was. Tommy calls, "Donny, I know where the guy is."

The guy was literally sitting in the windowsill. He had the window up and was sitting in the window. I mean, we knew where he was. We go up there and drag him out. Oh, I mean, escort him out nicely.

The whole time the girl was giving us a hard time, and we said, "I tell you what. We can go down and call your father," and, oh, did her attitude change quickly.

We had a guy, actually, we had two guys. Girl came out of the building, and she had a cart, and she took the cart all the way over to the East lot, and it was empty when Henry had her on camera. She packed this guy in the cart, crunched this guy in, packed him in with laundry and stuff and rolled it all the way to the back door.

"I can't let you in. You have a guy in the cart."

"No, I don't."

"Yeah, you do. I saw you on camera . . ."

"Well, why did you let me roll him all the way back over here?"

The guy obediently got out of the cart and left.

We had another guy. This was on my shift. He was with a group of girls, and I was watching them, and they put a dress on him and rolled his pants legs up and came through, and I told them, "You know what. I commend you for trying, but I can't let you in, Bubba."

"Well, but I'm trying to get in."

"Yeah, but the dress don't look all that great on you!"

A guy tried to get in on Halloween by putting on a wig.

I had one guy. Had to go up to the room and kick him out

when Perla was working. She said a boy was in a room. We'd had problems with this boy before. Knocked on the door, and he was sitting right on the bed.

I said, "You can't be up here man," this was like 11:30 at night.

The girl went off on me. "We've paid for this place and I want to bring him . . ."

I said, "We have rules around here, and after a certain time, he can't be up here." He wouldn't move, and I told him, "You can either get out of here on your own, or I can drag you out of here."

"Yes, sir," was his response, and he got up and walked out.

One time, the Fijis, maybe 15 to 17 of them came and did a raid, a panty raid. Ran through the building. I had guys running all through the building, knocking on doors and harassing girls. There was nothing I could do.

That's what this dorm is about. For ya'll to feel safe. If ya'll want to have boys running up and down the hall, you'd be at Jester. There really wadn't a lot of crazy things. This place ought to be proud there's never been anything bad happen.

You've heard about the story of the lady coming in, going into rooms and stealing things. We got pictures and gave them to police and everything. She just walked in and strolled the halls. She was a nice looking, normal looking lady, walking the halls calmly talking to people. The police said the good ones do that. She stole a laptop from a lounge.

One night, maybe I was working 3–11, maybe 7:30 or 8:30, a guy was over in the East parking lot, and I spotted him on the camera. I went over and he had a video camera. He told me he didn't have one, and I held him until the police got there. Then they found more videos the way he had been going into dorms and filming other girls. The security around here, Scottish Rite, is real good.

Haunted?

I took a group of 6-7 girls down to where the judge's office was, and we had that scary statue, and I was telling them ghost stories. I was in the back of the group and slammed the dividing door as we passed and they all screamed. I told them, "Come here and check this out, and they saw that statue and they didn't know what to do."

Then we have the East side ghost. One year I was working 11-7 at Christmas time, Robert can vouch for this. I got off from the elevator and looked down the hallway, and a little light went past, and I ran down there. Nothing. I turned right around and hooked it.

I was up on the floor one year with no girls and doing work, and I was supposed to be the only one in the building. I knew I was the only one in the building, when the elevator started moving. I was on two, and it was on four so I cut it off and came back down 'cause I didn't know what it was.

I told one girl about a ghost that goes around playing with doorknobs and the next morning she came down and told me someone had been playing with her doorknob. That's the East side ghost for you!

Tommy was up on four, and he said the East side door slammed. He was on the West side, but you'll have to take that up with him.

Maintenance Mishaps

I have one about Tommy, one of his little electrical mishaps. We were doing a sink job, changing a valve on the sink, and he didn't turn off the water so he took the valve off and "buuush," the water shot out and "poom" it hit the light bulb. He falls backwards. His eyes got like bug eyes. We quickly got the water turned off.

Did Elmer ever do anything funny?

(Elmer was the long-time and beloved bi-vocational minister/head of maintenance at SRD.)

What didn't Elmer do funny?

When he hooked up wires, it was a big thing for him. You know when you get the "pop." he'd sit there and say, "Heh, heh, heh. Did that one wrong."

On Elmer's famous grip ... He'd say, "Let's grip." He'd shake hands to see if he could out grip you.

On feeding the squirrels . . . He'd put a pecan in his mouth, and they would run up his leg to get it.

Oh, Rats!

Now's my chance to tell one on Brian . . . When he was fresh on the job, I called maintenance to remove a dead rat from my sliding storages in room 400.

Brian responded to my call, crawled into the small space and came backing out as fast as he could. (At this point in my story, Robert interjects quietly, "You got some gloves?" Obviously this story has followed Brian).

I look at Brian and tell him he needs to get the dead rat, and he looks back at me and says, "Do you have a glove or something?" I gave him a plastic shopping bag and showed him how to use it like a glove by putting it on, grabbing the rat and turning the bag inside out over the dead rat.

Talking about that rat story, one girl in another room lost her hamster and it got in some other girls' room, and both girls were up on their beds with shoes screaming. I'm on the ground looking for it, and it ran so fast it startled me and I jumped back and then they all screamed.

I had a cricket in a room, and these girls freaked out about that. As a matter of fact, I picked it up to show her, and she started crying, "I don't want to see, whahhhhhh!"

I had a couple girls when we had the old camera system who walked out of the back door, stopped over at the pool on the East side. They were just standing there laughing, and all of the sudden all you see is this girl falls flat on her back in the bushes and her friends are laughing at her. Later they came and asked if we had a tape of the event and borrowed it from us.

Tommy still doesn't remember any stories.

But I remember one he once told me . . .

One night I was on duty and I watched this boy climb the wall and go into a girl's window.

I went upstairs, found the room, and knocked on the door. When the girl answered, the boy was right there. He immediately started saying, "Yes, sir, I'll leave," and headed toward the door. I looked at him and said, "I think you can leave the same way you got in."

He gave me a stunned look but obediently climbed back out the window. Apparently going down was harder than coming up because he lost his grip and fell into the bushes.

—BRIAN, ROBERT, DONNY,
AND TOMMY (HEAD)
Current SRD Maintenance Men

Janet Janis was a security person in the early 1990's and possibly the first woman to fill this job. She recalls many Fiji pranks on her watch. In 1997, Joyce Krabe became the second female security guard and has since become the head of housekeeping.

Girls Will Be Girls!

And, Alice, Looking into the Past, Through the Looking Glass Was Surprised, Almost Unbelieving—

In May 1922, the *Sardine* was published for the first time. Every spring since then it has appeared to preserve fleeting memories of life in SRD. The title, *Sardine*, is usually taken for granted. Few girls bother to wonder how it was chosen. Those who do, presume it was taken from the combined initials SRD, and they are partly right.

The fall the dormitory opened, 306 girls moved in. So proud were they of their dormitory that all wore armbands initialed SRD through the entire school year. Since there were only about 2,000 students on the campus at that time, 306 girls wearing armbands became conspicuous. In a short while they were known and referred to as "Sardines." So when the dormitory voted on a name for the magazine which was to become an annual, *Sardine* was unanimously decided upon. And *Sardine* it remains today.

In the earlier days of the dormitory, the university itself did not provide so many cultural entertainments, so SRD put on several programs a year, many of which grew into traditions.

One of the loveliest events was the spring minuet. Half of the girls wore old-fashioned, wasp-waisted, full-skirted dresses made of tarletan.* The others, representing boys, were dressed in white satin tights and blouses. To the stately minuet, couples tripped, curtsied, and went under the arched arms of partners standing opposite.

Following the minuet, were presented charades, most of which represented some early American incident. The auditorium was always crowded, for Austin people begged for invitations.

Another custom was the Maypole dance, held on the west back lawn, the day of the Senior garden party. Girls in fluffy, full-skirted evening dresses wrapped the Maypole with ribbon streamers.

In the earlier days of the dormitory, lights were not left on all night as they now are. Many a term paper was written, and many an exam was studied for, by candlelight.

Usually semiannually, the dormitory in past years, would receive an invitation from the Austin Masons to give a program in Scottish Rite Cathedral. On the afternoon or night of the program, the chaperons heading the long line of dormitory girls, would march to the Cathedral. Ordinarily the girls merely sang, but on one memorable occasion, a skit was given, centered around a take-off on Mrs. Kauffman—which Mrs. Kauffman enjoyed as much as did the Masons.

Yes, SRD has had many traditions, which it seems a shame to let die. But since sorority and university programs often conflict, the directors of the dormitory do not wish to insist that the girls participate when they had rather do something else.

—*THE SARDINE*, 1938

*A muslin fabric that is thin and stiff with an open weave.

Patsy's Animals

Patsy Shurr, former receptionist at SRD, loved to go out in the yard to feed the squirrels and birds. She had them trained and would shake her keys while calling, "Squirrel, Sssquirrel." The squirrels would flock around her and she would feed them peanuts. Some would even take them from her hands.

One day she noticed that a woodpecker had started coming, and she wanted him to come closer so she could feed him, also. Without thinking, she called, "Pecker, pecker, pecker, pecker." The dorm window was open so the staff could hear what was going on outside. Someone ran to the door to stop her just as a man passed by on the sidewalk. Trying gently to explain the *faux pas*, the staffer said, "First of all I don't think he's going to come if you call and . . ."

Patsy never did really understand but gave up trying to entice the woodpecker and continued her daily feedings of all the other dorm animals.

—SUZIE HOLT
Administrator, 1992–present

Front Page News

Living in the "Pit" as it was known was a really fun experience. We were kind of cut off from the rest of the dorm so we formed quite a bond on our hall which always included a heavy dose of practical jokes.

For my birthday one year, my "friends" newspapered my room. When I opened the door, the entire room was about 3 feet deep in crushed newspaper in and on every available space. There was so much of it that once we pushed it out of the room, it filled the hallway.

—Candella Koomey Musselman
1974–1977

The Hand on the Hall

One evening we thought it would be funny to play a joke on our entire hall. My roommate had this motion-sensing hand that moved when you got close or touched it. About 11:00 P.M. we arranged some grungy blankets with the hand sticking out in the hall near the old elevator alcove. Then we told all of our neighbors that there was a homeless person down the hall.

They all came out to see and pretty soon the entire dorm had come to take a look. When they got close and touched it, the hand moved so they thought it was really a homeless person. Finally we started laughing and they said, "Are you just kidding?" Then we all laughed, everyone thought it was hilarious.

—Allison Horsley
2006–present

Some Statistics

The vanities left in boys' pockets by dormitory girls would supply Griffith Drug Co. for a year.

The candles used during exam week at the dormitory would, if all lit at once, be sufficient to signal Mars.

The candy lost on the A&M game, if all put together, would fill every room in the building.

The sugar taken from the tables in one week would be enough to sweeten our Jello for ten years.

The chiggers acquired at the picnic in Kauffman Grove would supply the zoo department for three sessions.

The silver taken from the tables by visitors would be enough to furnish weapons for a new World War.

The number of stamps used by Bertha May to send specials* to Harry would send the dormitory as far as Europe by parcel post.

—*THE ANNUAL SARDINE*
Volume 1, #1, 1922–1923

*The United States commenced special delivery service on October 1, 1885, and issued eleven collector-recognized stamps during its first 37 years. Beginning on July 12, 1922, modern transportation methods were shown on special delivery stamps. Special delivery mail was squeezed out by Express Mail on June 7, 1997.

A List of Demands

(Past, current and future SRD girls thank you!)

I was at SRD from September 1950–June 1954. In my first year I was one of those who slept on the porch of 2nd East. My roommate and I knew that we were to switch, but she would come in late, so I slept there the whole year. It was unheated, but I always had plenty of covers. By the time I moved, the sleeping porches had been enclosed and made into the sunrooms they are now. I learned to play bridge (Culbertson)* in the smoker and had my first success with a matron who bid 7 no and I had to play it. I will never forget that.

One of my best memories (among the hundreds) was in the spring of '54 when the Masonic Board for SRD met. A group of us decided we needed some changes at SRD, among them drink machines in the basement, laundry machines for our delicates which always came back starched from the laundry, and perhaps milk and snack machines were all on our list. I really felt sorry for those nice guys. We sat at different tables and after lunch (really good for a change) when we were asked if there was anything we might need to make the place better, we told them, even that a pool might be nice. Although we never saw these changes I later heard that future SRD generations benefited from our "meeting."

—BONNIE BAIN KILLAM
1950–1954

*Named for Ely Culbertson who learned to play bridge while in a Czarist jail. Of his bridge playing he said, "I was partly blamed for the fall of France in this war. [WWII] ... General Gamelin and other officers of the old French army were accused of playing bridge by the Culbertson system in time which might better have been spent in developing strategy to supplement the Maginot Line. In 1944 Culbertson presented his ideas for world peace known as The World Federation Plan.

—*DAILY TEXAN*, MARCH 7, 1944
reprinted with permission

SRD to Have First Dormitory Swimming Pool

"All in favor signify by raising their right hand."

Thus the Board of Directors of Scottish Rite Dormitory on February 28 made the rumor of a swimming pool for SRD a reality.

With construction beginning immediately, the pool will give residents an added recreational advantage, with a place for the girls and their guests to meet and have a good time without extra expense. The pool is scheduled for completion June 1.*

Scottish Rite Dormitory, dedicated in 1922, represents an investment of more than a million dollars. It owes its existence to the efforts of the late Sam P. Cochran of Dallas, who was instrumental in organizing the Scottish Rite Educational Association in 1920.

Mr. Cochran's dream was to establish a home at the university where the daughters and relatives of Masons would have the cultural and educational advantages that they had in their own homes.

When his goal was realized, Mr. Cochran gave to the dorm the Sue Higgins Cochran Memorial Library of 3,000 books. The collection contains many first editions, among which is a first edition of Mark Twain's *Roughing It*.

The Masons of Texas provided many other extras for SRD's residents. For instance, there is the SRD-owned greenhouse and 5-acre garden at the back of the site. An old tradition which is still maintained is "that a meal has never been served without the presence of fresh flowers on every table."

SRD is the only residential hall on the University of Texas campus with its own laundry, housed in the red brick annex at the back of the main dormitory. Handled by employes [sic], the laundry service is provided to each resident, and the only effort exerted by girls is the Sunday night chores of filling out the laundry list, sacking the clothes in the laundry bag, and making the short trip "out back" to pick up their clean starched clothes.

Hair dryers and sewing machines in the lounges, maid service, refreshments served every night during final exams, devotional services every Thursday night, educational and entertaining movies two or three times a month, and pajama parties every month are just a few of the facilities to which SRD women are accustomed.

First residents of Scottish Rite established many social traditions which are still observed. Among these are the formal dinners that are given on the important holidays—Hallowe'en, Thanksgiving, Valentine's, and Texas Independence Day. Christmas dinner, a special occasion, is served on Sunday night before the holidays. Dressed in semi-formal attire, the residents and their guests gather in the festively-decorated candle-lit dining hall for an old-fashioned feast of turkey and dressing.

Each January and May SRD seniors are honored with a luncheon and presented with an "SRD plate."

Most anticipated event of the year, however, is the SRD

spring formal. The residents, supervised by upperclass advisors and staff, plan the theme and make the elaborate decorations.

—Karen Wheeler
The Daily Texan, April 7, 1959
reprinted with permission

*The pool had male lifeguards until the 1970s!

Making a Splash

A day or two after we had all moved in, fall of 1977, the RA's told us we were going to have a fire drill. That evening around nine we were hurried outside. Our group from 2nd floor went outside to the pool area. I only knew my roommate at the time. We all had been moving in, saying goodbye to parents, and exploring the dorm. So, all of the faces were new.

We received the all clear to re-enter the building. Most girls were in robes over pajamas and anxious to get back to unpacking. One of the girls standing near me said, "I think I'll try out the pool!" Sure enough, there was a splash and this girl swam from one end of the pool to the other in her pajamas!

When Janet, my roommate, and I got back to our room there was a loud knock on the door. We opened it, and a wet girl flew into our room and asked to stand in a closet. With open mouths, we let her in. Not much later, there was another knock on the door. The RA asked to come in to see how our room was shaping up. Of course, she was looking for a wet college girl! No one gave away the secret in the closet.

Once our RA left, Martha introduced herself to us as our new next-door neighbor. That was the beginning of a long fun-filled relationship!

—Donna McDonald De Ron
1977–1979

UT Column

A female music student heard the tenderness of the harps

from above before going home for the Easter weekend. She had a bowlful of goldfish. She couldn't take them with her nor could she leave them to starve or suffocate in stale water. Everyone else went home, so the only thing to do was flush them down the toilet. It was a great example of humanity on Easter. The fish are probably still floating in the Scottish Rite Dorm pipes.

—CHARLIE SMITH
The Daily Texan, April 5, 1961
reprinted with permission

TV and Caviar

In the early sixties there were maids who actually lived at the dorm in the area that some might have known as the "Pit."

Down in the maids' quarters there were TVs which were still pretty scarce in the dorm at this time. In late 1960 and early 1961 the space launches were happening so we would go down to the maids' quarters to watch.

I remember seeing John Glenn go up, not even orbit, and come back to earth. It was an exciting thing to watch and was awe inspiring to us.

Another thing that left us in wonder was the caviar that was served at one of the dances. It was presented in a hollowed-out pineapple. There was much discussion about this strange new thing most of us girls from West Texas had only ever seen on TV.

—SYLVIA HULSEY WEST
1960–1964

Caught in the Act

During the mid '70s, streaking (running naked) was a popular activity on campus. One night we heard some girls say that two residents were streaking through the main living room wearing only paper bags on their heads. We all ran downstairs to look and saw them just as they were running back up the stairs. We guessed who one of them was right

away because she had been to the lake that day and had
badly sunburned legs. The paper bag on her head must have
obscured her vision because as she ran up the stairs she,
tripped, fell, and broke her leg.

I wonder what she told the doctor?

—BECKY SHANNON EADDY
1973–1975

More Broken Bones

One night an SRDine wanted to leave the dorm after the
front door was locked for the night, so she decided to jump out
the window of a first floor sunroom. The distance to the
ground was more than she had expected and instead of a fun
night on the town, she got a broken leg.

—ANNONYMOUS
1972–1975

Bored Co-eds Bring Fame to SRD

It was fall of 1955, my freshman year at UT and SRD. To
be exact, it was Texas-OU weekend. Back then, we had strict
rules regarding hours to be in, and permission from parents
was required for weekends away.

My friend Joan Jordan, and I did not have permission to go
to Dallas and felt a little out of sorts to be stuck in Austin
when all the fun seemed to be in Dallas.

We happened to note that Charlton Heston was coming to
the Paramount Theater in Austin for the world premiere of the
movie, *Lucy Gallant*. We thought our weekend could be sal-
vaged if we could get Mr. Heston to be our guest at SRD for
dinner.

Friday afternoon, we called the theater and a few phone
calls later reached his manager. He said if we would call back
Monday at 11:00 A.M. he would let us know for certain if they
could come for dinner Monday night.

We did not tell a soul what we had done because if this little project failed, it would forever be a secret between Joan

and me. Since I had an 11:00 class, Joan made the call to Mr. Heston's manager and was told that he, Mr. Heston, and one more guest from the Paramount staff would be glad to be our guests that evening.

I arrived at the dorm shortly after 12:00 P.M. and now we were panicked. We figured we better tell the dorm mother first what we had done.

Her first reaction was, "Oh my goodness, all the table-cloths (we always had white linen tablecloths on Sunday) are in the laundry." We assured her that was not a problem; we had not promised tablecloths.

Next, she began to talk about how we would put him at the head table and who would get to sit there. We said, "Oops, he and his entourage are our guests; we are paying for their meals, and we want them to sit at our table with our friends." She agreed and that afternoon we invited the lucky people who would join us.

Shortly before dinner, we went to the front lawn to await our hero, and still a little nervous that he might not actually show up. Right on the dot, 6:00, he and his entourage arrived. Meanwhile, they had all the SRD residents standing at dinner waiting for a bit longer than usual. They had no clue what was happening.

After the introductions on the front lawn, we made our way to the dining room. Our regular table was at the East end of the room, so we, of course, made our grand entrance at the West end so we could show our prize to the entire room. As we entered, we could hear the murmurs, "It's Charlton Heston; no, it can't be; yes, it is!"

We had a most delightful time with Mr. Heston. He was especially impressed with our waiter and told us all about how he had waited tables while attending Northwestern University.

He answered the many curious questions about this person and that person in Hollywood.

All in all he was a delightful guest. I don't know what his take on the evening was, but I do know that he absolutely made the entire fall semester a success for two young freshmen!

—Betty Jordan Boynton
1955–1959

Star Delights SRD Diners

What causes more squeals of delight than baked Alaska for dessert at SRD? Charlton Heston!

To the surprise of the girls chattering in the dining room, Mr. Heston was proudly escorted to dinner by two grinning freshmen, Joan Jorden and Betty Jorden. They called him Tuesday afternoon and asked him to have dinner at SRD.

His coming was a complete surprise to all but eight girls, two counselors, and a few of the waiters, who took pictures of the movie star.

The girls started squealing with delight when he walked the length of the dining room trying to find a place to sit with his manager, Bob Bixler; the manager of the Paramount Theater, Bob Hellums; and their two proud escorts.

One of the lucky girls that sat at his table sighed, "He was a real gentleman, and his voice, and those hands!"

—*The Daily Texan*, 1956
reprinted with permission

Mrs. Fowler's Cleaning Frenzy

In 1993 I stayed at SRD for freshman orientation in a sunroom on First West. When I was settling in and preparing to take a nap, I noticed there was a bug in the sheets of the bed. It was small and dead, but I decided to tell housekeeping anyway.

What happened next was a hysterical whirlwind that showed me just how dedicated to my comfort they were at SRD. I was quickly escorted out of the room and told to wait in the living room while they dealt with the situation. All the while apologies were expressed for any distress this event had caused.

Mrs. Fowler, the head of housekeeping, came to change the sheets herself and inspect the room for any other pests. It's possible that the room was even exterminated before I was allowed to return. This kind of dedication is what made Mrs. Alice Fowler such a wonderful Head of Housekeeping for the 24 years she served SRD.

—Amie Stone King
1993–1997

SNAKE!

My friend Mary lived in the area that we nicknamed the "Pit," which was on the ground level and had once been quarters for live-in workers. In that area there were only a couple of student rooms, but Mary liked it because it was very quiet. One day upon entering her room, Mary found a rather large snake and was terrified. She quickly went to the dorm mother and reported the snake but the dorm mother didn't seem alarmed and asked Mary, "Well, what do you want me to do about it?" Finally one of the maintenance men removed it, but I don't think Mary ever felt safe in that room again.

—ANONYMOUS
1972–1975

Pickles

Of the many chores that waiters are required to perform, saving the milk is one of the least fun. Open the dispenser, heave the unruly bag into a crate, and haul it back to the refrigerator until it is hauled, heaved, and returned to the dispenser the next day. And don't forget that this happened three times for 2%, skim, and chocolate. After one tiring day, I performed this duty yet again, and when I got into the refrigerator, placed the crate on top of a five gallon bucket. I have no idea exactly what occurred next, expect to say that a pungent odor of vinegar was in the air and I was leaping back to get out of the flood. About half the pickles and all the juice spilled from the bucket after it toppled and the lid popped off. Of course I then had to clean up the mess and endure the teasing since the aroma had spread throughout the kitchen and attracted a lot of attention.

—MATT KING
Waiter/Dishwasher, 1995–1996

The SRD Mouse Trap

One year Patsy Shurr, the dorm receptionist, told the girls

that SRD had a mouse problem and they were all over the place. Her advice for solving the problem was to put Butch, the dorm cat, in their rooms. This seemed like a good idea to the girls so they summoned Butch and set him on a mouse's trail. With haste Butch caught the mouse and proceeded to do something the girls hadn't counted on. He crunched the mouse and ate it—in their room! Thoroughly disgusted, the girls fled.

Patsy loved to tell the story to everyone, including the new residents, stressing, "He just crunched down. Right there!"

—SUZIE HOLT
Administrator, 1992–present

No Screaming on the Hall

During my freshman year at UT, I lived on the 2nd floor of SRD. One Sunday night at 9:00 or 10:00 my roommate, friends, and I were laughing really hard and being silly. Suddenly my friend Barbara announced that she heard a sound like a monster, so for fun we all screamed. The next thing we knew there was a knock on our door, and a policeman was standing there. We assured him we were not drinking or anything, just having fun. He said, "I understand someone screamed here," so I explained that my friend said she heard a monster sound and that was why we had screamed. He looked at me like, "Ya'll are in college?" Then he advised us not to scream anymore. It was kind of embarrassing at the time, but funny to think of later.

—CANDELLA KOOMEY MUSSELMAN
1974–1977

Itty Bitty Living Space

In the spring semester of my first year at SRD, I changed roommates, and had to take my new roommate's priority. My new roommate was someone I knew from Longview, Texas, and we had gone to Kilgore Junior College together. I moved out of my room on 3rd West and down into the basement. The basement was a long room, with rows of beds that looked like army cots. It had housed the workers and housekeepers (women from German families who stayed at SRD and kept house or worked in the laundry or kitchen). We absolutely loved it.

At first there were three of us down there in an enormous room, with no phone. It was very quiet, somewhat dimly lit, and poorly furnished.

At mid-semester a room became vacant on 2nd East. My roommate (Gay Correll) and I moved from a huge basement room to a Trundle. A Trundle was a room shared by two people. One bed slid underneath the other, higher bed in the morning. At night, when we pulled the bed out, we could not get the door open.

I slept on the trundle bed and Gay slept on the higher bed. Our window looked north over the swimming pool and down the hall, the window looked out past the parking lot to the Presbyterian Seminary.

The next year, we had higher priorities and we got a room on second East, across and down the hall a bit from our trundle.

At the beginning of that year, I was in my room, having just moved in, when Gay opened the door with complete dismay on her face. Her father had been bringing her down to school and along the way, some spark had come up through the floor boards of the back seat and the resulting fire had completely destroyed all her clothes. Everything was burned up—a real disaster for any college coed, and especially for Gay. She had lots and lots of clothes.

She secured emergency funding from the University and gift certificates from stores on the "Drag," such as Yarings, Marie Antoinette, the Cadeau, Scarbroughs, and a shoe store.

I spent the week of registration going with her from store to store, trying on dresses and buying new clothes. She got an entire new wardrobe from the kindness and generosity of the University and merchants.

She became known as the Girl Whose Clothes Burned Up. People would stop by our room just to talk about the disaster. We made many new friends that year.

—JANE ARCHER FEINSTEIN
1964–1966, 1967

Dining, Biking, and the Long Kiss Goodnight

CCB's (chocolate crumble balls) on "some" Sunday lunches but not all—I'm convinced they used the principal that intermittent reward increases behavior, i.e., having those fabulous CCB's "only sometimes" meant no one ever missed Sunday lunches. And sitting in the alcove windows when the 5th floor study hall was empty—singing—looking way down over the beautiful gardens in the back.

And, having the first bicycle at SRD that fall of '66. No one else had one, but I had to have it to save walking all the way to the Music Building next to the Littlefield Fountain (because of my hips).

That winter, I remember the boys throwing snowballs at me—a moving target. In the spring, my music major friend, Ruth, started parking the second bicycle behind SRD. Her hips were fine, but she thought the bike was a pretty good idea.

And Mrs. McConnell, who could forget her? And as our room was right over the front door on the second floor, I remember all the boys and girls standing out under our open window at curfew "smooching." I didn't mind the smooching, just the noise when I was trying to sleep.

Most of all, about SRD, I remember Betty Sue, my roommate, and my best friend!

—Cathy Marable
1965–1967

What a Place

They ironed our clothes, changed our sheets, cleaned our rooms, and fed us wonderful food. When my friends tried to get me to move into an apartment with them, I said, "You gotta be kidding. Why would I want to leave all this?"

SRD was a wonderful place, especially to a girl from a small town in South Texas. When I attended one of my first classes at Batts, it was culture shock since there were more people in the class than in my whole town. It is amazing that my mother even allowed me to go to UT because the Whitman incident happened one week after I attended freshman orientation.

On my first weekend at UT, my future husband and I were saying goodnight outside SRD along with about 25 other couples, and after we broke our embrace, he stepped back and said, "Now, what was your name again?" The other couples actually stopped kissing and stared at us. We had been dating over 1½ years at that point, and I wanted to strangle him.

For the most part I followed the rules. I remember sneaking out through a basement window one night and letting Dick in through one of the basement windows to visit while I practiced piano (there was a piano in one of the old maids' rooms). One night Kay, my roommate, and I decided it would be fun to throw water balloons from our 4th floor window down onto the kissing couples. That caused quite a stir!

Kay and I loved CCB's, and we would ask all the other girls, "Do you want your CCB?" Sometimes if we were lucky we'd get three each.

My daughter Julie spent a summer at SRD, and she loved it. I was surprised by how everything was still the same.

—MALDA MAYO BURNS
1966–1969

The Sprinkler System

Ms. McConnell was the matron of SRD when I was there. At that time SRD had a lawn sprinkler system, which may have been one of the first put in anywhere.

The Sigma Nus, a confederate-themed fraternity, always delivered invitations to their formals on horseback and in full regalia.

This particular evening, they rode up in uniforms and on horses to SRD. Ms. McConnell turned on the sprinkler system because she didn't want the horses on her lawn. She was famous for using the sprinklers as a weapon, especially during panty raids!

—SYLVIA HULSEY WEST
1960–1964

No Special Treatment

Ms. Dehoney, the SRD matron, was always partial to the sorority girls. She would turn a blind eye if they came in late, etc. I had done Rush but decided not to pledge so I was not one of her chosen girls.

Watching this special treatment occur was very frustrating, so a group of us got together and had a little meeting and put a stop to it. Even the dean of women at UT, Dean Gabauer, helped us with our plight.

I know I drove Ms. Dehoney crazy, but in my mind it was all about fairness. After deciding not to rush, I became a charter member of the Women's Independent Campus Assn., which lasted for quite a while.

—JERRY COCHRAN MOORE
1944–1945

Jerry Cochran Moore was a member of *Who's Who at UT* along with Rooster Andrews.

Rooster Andrews attended the University of Texas at Austin from 1941–1946 where he served as the team manager for athletics. Fondly labeled the "All American Water Boy," Rooster also served as the team manager for the College All Stars from 1942–1946. His sporting goods store is a family-owned business, incorporated in 1971.

Dube's Dolls

My last year at SRD, I was an RA. We called ourselves Dube's Dolls, created a dorm-wide newsletter called Dube's Dispatch and had T-shirts made. Mr. Dube was the sweet older caretaker whom we really liked. I have the happiest memories of living at SRD.

Times were a lot different back then, we didn't go out a lot, we didn't have cars, we stayed in the dorm pretty much every night and studied up in the 5th floor study hall where it was spooky and creepy, and the desks were in the little cubby holes. On Saturday nights the guys would come over, and we would order pizza. I can remember sitting on the light blue sofas in the Rec Room watching *Saturday Night Live* when it was brand new. These are such wonderful memories.

—PAM BLOOM CAMOSY
1973–1976

TV Bonding

One of the greatest memories I have of SRD is becoming really close friends with my other 4th floor dorm-mates, Tammy Borsellino, Vera Miller Taboada, and Kim Matthews. We always ate dinner and watched television together. It was at a time when none of our rooms had cable connections so we all hung out in the 4th floor TV lounge. It was a great way to get to know one another. One night we decided to take Salsa dancing lessons and then go to a Salsa dance club. It was so much fun! Salsa dancing became our outlet from studying that semester!

—NICOLLE SKYIEPAL
1995–1997, 2000–2001

SRD Memories

SRD was truly my "home away from home" for the four years I lived there. Each time I walked through the back door after being gone for the summer, I immediately felt at home. The memories and friends made at SRD will last a lifetime.

I think we all took it for granted how good we had it at SRD. Anytime a friend or classmate came through the front doors, they always said, "Wow, you live here?!" and then proceeded to tell me some story about their horrible experiences at their dorm or run down apartment in which they were living.

Christmastime at SRD was always a treat. The white lights created such a magical look. The annual Christmas dinner was something to look forward to before finals started, and a reason to get dressed up. The CCB's were excellent, of course. And, it was so much fun anticipating the final outcome of the hall decorating contest.

Although squirrels are seen as the "official" SRD mascots, for my friends and me, Butch the cat is the unofficial mascot. He was so skinny that we always wanted to feed him—until we saw one of the waiters bring him leftovers one night after dinner. Then we knew he was being sufficiently spoiled.

Home football games. I never tired of seeing the sea of burnt orange shirts, denim skirts and cowboy hats depart SRD for the stadium, and then ecstatically return after yet another Longhorn win!

Each year, there were countless 2:00 A.M. fire alarm wake up calls due to girls overcooking popcorn. Really, girls, it's not that difficult. "You push the button labeled 'popcorn,' and wait for the microwave to finish." Looking back, it's funny to think about all those girls standing around outside in the middle of the night in their pajamas, but at the time—incredibly annoying.

Throughout the years, Mary Mazurek and Susie Holt were always willing to lend a sympathetic ear to us girls when we had a roommate problem or just needed to vent about school. Thank you ladies!

My girlfriends and I were probably one of the last group of SRD graduates—girls who lived at SRD all four years. Our graduation gifts of SRD cookbooks will be treasured and relied upon for many years to come.

Graduation in 2004 was bittersweet. We were all excited to graduate, but sad to leave SRD. Moving out was such an odd feeling. I actually had to clear out my storage unit—something that had not been done in three years. I still keep in touch with my SRD girls and enjoy using the cookbook when I need a CCB fix. To my 4th floor girls, Jenny, Mary Alice, Llewyn, Erin, Tori, and Michelle, thank you for your friendship and the magical memories.

—CARRIE NELSON
2000-2004

Chilling

One of my favorite things about SRD was the CCBs! The few days during the year that CCBs were on the menu were the best days of the year. No matter how badly my day was going, a CCB* always made everything better.

Also, was I the only person who was always terrified to go into the attic storage space area?! It didn't matter what time of day or night it was, I always felt like something was hiding around each corner waiting to grab me . . . scary!

—KATHRYN LEACH VAN ZANDT
1993–1996

*A CCB, also known as a Chocolate Crumble Ball, is a ball of vanilla ice cream rolled in crushed Hydrox chocolate cookies and then topped with homemade hot fudge sauce.

Squirrel Interrupted

One day I was sitting in the office and this girl came in and very calmly said, "I have just been attacked by a squirrel." And you know, at SRD we have a thing for squirrels with the fountain and the statue and everything. I said, "Honey, what?" and she said, "I was just attacked by a squirrel." and she lifted up her pant leg and she was bleeding. The maintenance men came, cleaned it up and put a bandage on it, but then we determined that she needed to go to the Health Center

The UT Health Center personnel told her she did not need the rabies shots, but her mother got a little excited and called Brackenridge Hospital. They told her she did need the shots. She actually got halfway through a round of rabies shots before she was informed that there has never been a case of rabies in the U.S. from a squirrel.

The funniest thing about this squirrel attack was that the administration got very excited and called the maintenance men, and they came with nets and everything. This squirrel, I mean, I'm not kidding, I've never seen a squirrel with this expression on his face. He was like, "Bring it on." There was a standoff between the maintenance guys and the squirrel. Of course, they couldn't catch it so there is still an attack squirrel out there somewhere living in the front yard of SRD.

—TERRI SHEARER
Resident Director, 2006–2007

SRD won an *Austin Chronicle*'s Best of Austin award for "Best Obscure Animal Statue" for the squirrel statue by the fountain.

—THE AUSTIN CHRONICLE
September 24, 1999
reprinted by permission

Things My Daughter Learned While at SRD . . .

How to remove 44 ounces of bright blue Sonic Ocean Water drink from brand new cream-colored Berber carpeting: *Use lots of water, towels, and elbow grease.*

How to get one huge pothole and numerous small ones in the east parking lot repaired quickly: *Leave a note in the suggestion box that says, "Please repair the Mother of All Potholes and her children!"*

How to marry an SRD waiter: *Never say never.*

—ANNETTE STONE
SRD Mother

UT Column

A boy was caught unaware when he entered Scottish Rite Dormitory to pick up his date this week. A girl he knew casually sauntered up and said, "Hi! Let's go make love."

The boy stammered something about having a date.

"Oh, come on," the girl coaxed.

Again the boy was speechless.

"What's the matter?" the girl badgered. "Aren't you my lover?"

Pushed to the breaking point the boy replied, "Oh, yes, but only on MWF. It's Thursday, you know."

—CHARLIE SMITH
The Daily Texan, May 5, 1961
reprinted with permission

Butch

In the fall of 1994 a small midnight-black kitten wandered

up to the dorm. He was friendly and sweet. We all formed an immediate attachment, but no one more than the dorm receptionist at the time, Patsy Shurr. She was a known cat lover, and when she saw the precious little black fur ball she couldn't resist.

Patsy succeeded in having his neutering and shots paid for by the dorm, and thus began his official tenure as the SRD cat. Butch, as he was named by Patsy because she thought he needed a virile name being a male cat at a girls dorm, was a loyal friend to all and took immense pleasure in hanging out in girls' rooms, although this often left him stranded.

I was awakened one night by a terrible yowling sound in the hallway only to find Butch standing by the elevator begging to go outside. Another resident had put him in the hall but failed to completely release him from the confines of the dorm.

Not wanting to go all the way to the ground floor, and walk down the maintenance hallway in my pajamas, I summoned the elevator and placed Butch inside. Then I pressed the ground floor button, returned to my room and called the maintenance man on duty to let him know Butch was on his way down in the elevator.

Butch remained a faithful dorm friend for almost thirteen years. In early April of 2007 he passed away and went to join Patsy who died in 2005. We all think it was probably a very happy reunion.

—AMIE STONE KING
1993–1997

Keils' Wheelchair

Kathy Keils stepped off the shuttle one day and was struck by a bicyclist which probably contributes to her dislike of them to this day!

She broke her ankle pretty severely and got a motorized wheelchair. The girls on 3 East enjoyed racing down the hallway in that thing.

—ANNA HOLMGREEN
1976–1980

Attic Anna

One night an SRD resident named Anna did not return to the dorm. Her friend became very worried because usually she would call if she was staying out all night. After frantically searching the dorm, her friend called the police. The next morning Anna strolled into the dorm to a relieved yet angry welcome. She claimed to have been studying in her attic closet all night. We thought that sounded strange, and we eventually found out that she had stayed the night with her boyfriend. The next day there was an article in *The Daily Texan* about her disappearance and strange explanation. After that, she was known as "Attic Anna."

—ANONYMOUS
1972–1975

Boo!

At the beginning of the 2006–2007 school year there was a little man who hid in the hedges and jumped out at passing girls. It was never determined if he was a homeless person or a fraternity pledge required to frighten SRD girls as part of a hazing ritual. He came back two or three times and each time the girls would come in laughing about the "man jumping out at people from the bushes." Each time we called maintenance and he ran away.

—TERRY SHEARER
Resident Director
2006–2007

Just Being Girls?

Who could forget late night road trips to Mrs. Johnson's donuts, the weekend we thought we lost Bing Crosby's daughter (who of course grew up to shoot JR), or the group of non-Greek friends who countered the rush madness by forming our own sorority-Sigma Rho Delta chapter of which I am pledge president for life. And what about finding the low spots in the lawn as early as January because out of the wind you could just bear to sunbathe!

Then there were girls calling down to the RA on duty to describe their blind dates using the "dessert" code, where the best dates were "Baked Alaska." Or, just the ordinary Friday nights with all the doors on 3rd West open to the hallway, Dolly Parton's *Two Doors Down* blasting on someone's stereo and everyone running around in towels getting ready to go out, singing and laughing together; how I still know the piccolo parts to all the Longhorn Band songs to this day because of the band member on my floor, and still thinking about yelling "FLUSH!" before flushing the toilet so not to scald the person in the shower; leading your Dad off the elevator yelling "Man On The Floor"; or after gathering around the "smoker" TVs to watch the Heisman Ceremonies, then running with lots of girls from the dorm out to the lawn to see the tower lit in the orange #1, taking pictures and then being drawn with thousands of others to sing and dance in front of the tower to celebrate with the chant of "Earl won the Heisman!"

Residents often used the RAs on duty to screen their blind dates. We would pretend that someone was calling down to inquire about the next dessert on the menu when in reality they were describing their blind dates. We would use food analogies to let them know how attractive we thought the date was and sometimes were called upon to make excuses for the girl! The best dates were always Baked Alaska.

Mary Francis Crosby came to stay at the dorm in one of the 2nd East suites. She was younger than the typical freshman and, of course, caused quite a buzz. The RAs were a little concerned when she wasn't in the dorm for several days and hadn't signed out on her attendance card as was still required for residents at the time. Then we realized, upon seeing the show on television, that she had been home taping the annual *Bing Crosby Family Christmas Special*! By 1979 she was a star in the TV show *Dallas* as Kristin, the character who shot JR.

One of my favorite times was the annual dinner with the Board of Directors. There was one man who always sat down and played the grand piano for us.

I lived in a sunroom single so when the double doors were

left open, you could see my door from all the way down the hall. Instead of a small message board, I purchased and hung a 2x3 ft. artist sketchpad on my door. Those pages became a wonderful montage of notes, drawings, and running commentary. It was a chat room before there was an internet! I think the page that drew the most attention, and could be seen all the way down the hall from the moment you turned off the elevator, was left shortly after the made-for-TV movie about Charles Manson aired on April 1, 1976. Someone scrawled in dripping red paint, the words, HELTER SKELTER!

There were always pranksters in the dorm, shortsheeting beds, putting packing peanuts in everything. One time some girls completely emptied one of the sunrooms—not even leaving the bed—and locking the door behind them! The creepiest was slipping your feet under the crisp dorm-laundered sheets and hitting the bristles of a hairbrush! That'll get you out of bed quick! The statues were often dressed and decorated, especially during the long nights of exams when even the kitchen's late evening snacks weren't enough to keep us occupied.

As an RA, I saw a lot of things. Because the room doors opened across the sink, it was easy to fill a sink with ice and beverages and not get caught. When the door opened you couldn't see the sink. In the days of vinyl LPs, you could fill the cardboard album sleeve with shaving cream, slide the edge under a door and then step on the album to blow shaving cream all across a locked room! Many a time we would find the inside of the bathroom stalls papered with cutouts from *Playgirl* magazine, and one evening I came home to find the smoker Christmas tree completely adorned with tampon ornaments.

—CANDY ANDREWS
1975–1979

Our Neighbors

Great white columns peeping through a myriad of trees—that's SRD

The grounds on which the dormitory is built are among the most beautiful of any dormitory anywhere. Rolling, velvety, green lawns, shrubs, and rose gardens surround the building. The grounds are like a vast colonial garden, even to the cobblestone walks leading up to the doorsteps.

The "backyard" is almost as well known as the front. Many a young man had been enticed out into the moonlight to sit on the benches under the trees there. It's a funny thing, but it is very probable that more stars have been counted from beneath those trees, more dreams dreamed, and more moons looked at from those benches than from anywhere else on the campus of the university. The backyard, you know, stretches out into a flat xpanse [sic] for a way, and then it dips suddenly into a little ravine—and what a ravine! More moons, more stars, and more dreams from more benches.

And our neighbors! Three phases of education (?) are represented in the surroundings of SRD Phi Gams, the church,and the president's home. First on our right, the Phi Gamma Delta boys, and do they enjoy their proximity to the dorm? Do they? You know, that's a swell roof they have on their house, not mentioning the sleeping porches. The sun baths are excellent there, and they do say that field glasses can be focused perfectly from those heights. Well, maybe—but that's enough of the Phi Gams, even though they do invite us to slip out of the dormitory after 11:00 and "go over and listen to the music at the church."

The Church. All Saints Chapel is just in front of the dormitory. It's terribly convenient for the Episcopalian girls to go to church on Sunday. Who says there is no air of refinement near SRD?

And heavy, heavy hangs over our head on our left. The home of President H.Y. Benedict of the University of Texas. It's a pretty home, too, and don't you think he chose a nice location for it? But when we get to talking about President Benny that always leads sooner or later to the thought that he is president of that school to which our mothers and fathers sent us to get educated—thus we recall studying. Let us stop there.

Well, there you are. That's the way the surroundings of SRD are. What's that definition? Oh—a piece of land surrounded entirely by nice neighbors and beautiful scenery—that's SRD

—*THE SARDINE*, 1932

Top View

An elderly friend of mine, now deceased, told me that during the 1930s when she lived at SRD, girls would sunbathe on the roof of the recreation room wearing only their panties. Guess nothing is new under the sun.

—ANONYMOUS
1972–1975

Touches of Home

I remember the first time I visited SRD as a junior in high school . . . and immediately knew it was the place for me. How it felt like home—safety and comfort in the midst of this teeming mass of people at UT, a home base to branch out and explore from.

I loved that it was girls only, so if you needed to run down the hall in your T-shirt to iron something, you could. That we could stay up late in the TV room in our PJs talking and watching movies, order pizza and not feel self-conscious about chowing down.

I loved the history of the building, how it felt to walk in after class. How they looked out for you with sack lunches if you had class, and snacks in the afternoon . . . and who am I kidding? I loved housekeeping! I loved pressed sheets every week and that we got to know our hall's housekeeper over the year.

I loved sit-down Sunday dinners, chicken crepes, and CCBs. But most of all, I loved the friends I made at SRD . . . from my BFF—still 15 years later . . . to my freshman year potluck roomie who lives in Virginia now with her husband and three children (and lived on dill pickles and cheese the year we roomed together) . . . to the girls on my hall when I was an RA . . . these girls made my UT experience . . . and a few contributed to who I am today . . . and I wouldn't have it any other way. Thanks, SRD!

—SABRA PHILLIPS
1992–1994, 1996–1997

A Continued Connection

At SRD, my first room was 319. My roommate was from Odessa. She was a science major and went with a lab assistant who had transferred to UT, just as she had, from Odessa Junior College. She talked me into cutting her naturally curly hair one night, even though I certainly protested against it. The next morning early I awoke to see her sitting in front of the mirrors fixing and fixing her hair. I could sense the displeasure. I never cut anyone else's hair again. She was a good sport. Later I was in her wedding.

Forty years or so after I lived in SRD, Elizabeth Avant, my daughter's best friend, moved into SRD. She lived in 319. To commemorate the irony and to see if my spirit still lived in 319, I visited her one Wednesday night just to see my old room. It was completely changed. They had renovated the room and removed the pullout mirrors, changed the closets and chests, and painted the room some garish color. I was stunned at the difference.

That same night, I visited the SRD librarian, Pam Archer. She had been my running partner back in the 1970s. Now she was a mom and I was a mom with grown children. And we had met again in a place in which we never thought our paths would cross.

—JANE ARCHER FEINSTEIN
1964–1966, 1967

We Won't Forget . . .

Eating breakfast with our eyes closed . . . watching avidly for the arrival of the postman . . . candlelight dinners, with emphasis on the "Sand Bars" . . . the dull thud experienced when we see the five minute warning flicker of entrance lights at 10:55 every night . . . pajama parties in the ballroom . . . the "relief line" to get milk and crackers during the hungry hours at exam time . . . dormitory formals—lilting lyrics and light laughter . . . the sunstroke addicts who cluster on the rear lawn cum spring . . . the pitch-dark attic with its shafts of light from student lamps . . . serenades—whether Christmas carols or political hoi polloi . . .

—*THE SARDINE*
Volume 17, 1939

Homage to My Friends

I remember . . .
- the Wine and Cigarettes Club that met on the 5th floor.
- the scary "dead person" on the wall behind the gate in the elevator, complete with blood dripping all the way from 4th floor down to the basement.
- the walls moving and the floor being slanted after a "graduation party" in an RA's room.
- birthday parties and wedding showers in suite 6 and the Rec Room.
- matching room décor at SRD and at home.
- sharing a practice room in the "Pit."
- deciding it would be more fun to have a slumber party in each other's rooms after watching late night horror movies.
- scheduling classes so as not to miss favorite TV shows.
- small graduation parties in the TV lounge on 4th floor.
- movies shot at 3:00 A.M. during dead week boredom.
- staying up all hours of the night working on Christmas Hall Decorations and then having to guard them from creeping marauders.
- deciding we'd had enough of hall decorations and that we'd make a donation to the Scottish Rite Hospital instead.
- balloons left over from a Valentine's dance tied to a waiter's bicycle.
- the smell of incense mixed with coffee and York Peppermint Patties.
- driving, talking, and eating for hours.

—ANONYMOUS

Mrs.

It's just amazing how much a place can stay the same over

the years. It's very comforting that SRD hasn't changed since the changes on campus are mind-boggling. My mother, my older sister, and I all lived at SRD. One of the things I remember most was the "Engagement Circle." We would call a group of girls together whenever someone became engaged and then light a candle. As we passed the candle around the circle we would sing *Let Me Call You Sweetheart*. When the song ended, we passed the candle until the girl who was engaged held it and blew it out. Only the circle organizers knew who was engaged so it was a surprise to all the other girls.

— LAURA ELLIS KEIVENHOVEN
1978–1982
— DOROTHY BITHAY ELLIS
1943–1944

Mourning the Loss

The most devastating time at SRD was the second Christmas I was in the dorm. Four girls from the dorm were killed on their way home from school for the holidays. They were all from around Corpus Christi, I think. The news came back to us before I left for the holidays. A drunk driver had hit them head on and killed them instantly. We were especially anguished because the driver of the car was Marilyn. People had started rumors about her that fall, and she had had a bad time with gossip before she left. When we came back from Christmas, we had a candlelight ceremony in the Rec Room. It was packed and very beautiful. The entire dorm grieved, and I imagine the people who had gossiped felt awful indeed.

— JANE ARCHER FEINSTEIN
1964–1966, 1967

5th Victim Claimed
4 UT Coeds Die in Wreck

Four girl members of the University of Texas Longhorn Band were killed near Houston Friday evening in a two-car head-on crash on Interstate Highway 10.

The lone occupant of the other car involved was also killed.

The University of Texas band is to appear at the Bluebonnet Bowl football game Saturday between the University of Texas and the University of Mississippi.

Dead at the scene were:

—Marilyn Lundell, 20, a junior at UT living at Scottish Rite Dormitory; her home address is Box 325, Freer.

—Kathy Sue Billiot, 18, a freshman living at 210 W. 27th St.; her home address is 2811 Rose Ave., Groves.

—Jennifer Susan Bomar, 19, a sophomore living at SRD; her home address is 10715 Lansdowne, Houston.

—Jo Ann Slaughter, 20, a sophomore living at SRD; her home address is 517 Pugh, Woodsboro.

—Carl Francis Wright, driver of the second car involved in the collision, of 149½ San Felipe, Sealy.

Houston sources said the girls' car was traveling west on IH 10 and the Wright car east on the highway.

That the four girls were all members of the Longhorn Band was confirmed in Houston by John Edmunds, assistant band director.

The accident happened at 7:30 P.M., seven miles west of Brookshire, near Sealy.

—Tom Barry
Austin American-Statesman
©1966, reprinted with permission

Scottish Rite Dormitory Memorial

Thursday, January 5, 1967
11:30 P.M.

MEMORIAL SERVICE
Marilyn Lundell
Jennifer Susan Bomar
Jo Anne Slaughter
Cathy Sue Billiot

ORGAN PRELUDE—Patricia Ann Ogle

READING THE TWENTY THIRD PSALM—Joyce Bowen

BIOGRAPHICAL STATEMENT—Mrs. F.C. McConnell

CANDLE LIGHTING CEREMONY:

Patricia Krause	Marilyn Lundell
Judy Catherine Miller	Jo Anne Slaughter
Carol Cone	Jennifer Susan Bomar
Jeanie Lane	Cathy Sue Billiot

THE APOSTLES' CREED—Recited by all

I believe in God the Father Almighty, Maker of heaven and earth; and in Jesus Christ his only Son our Lord; who was conceived by the Holy Ghost, born of the Virgin Mary, suffered under Pontius Pilate, was crucified, dead, and buried; the third day he rose again from the dead, he ascended into heaven, and sitteth at the right hand of God the Father Almighty; from thence he shall come to judge the quick and the dead. I believe in the holy Ghost; the holy catholic Church; the communion of saints; the forgiveness of sins; the resurrection of the body; and the life everlasting. Amen.

THE LORDS PRAYER—Acapella—Cathy Ann Marable

ORGAN POSTLUDE—Patricia Ann Ogle

A Wedding Story

I was a student at the University of Texas from 1961 through 1965 and was first a dishwasher and then a waiter at SRD from 1963–1965.

Many things were different back in those days. First and foremost dining was by seated service for the noon and evening meals (breakfast was buffet). Waiters were scheduled to work 2 meals a day but were entitled to eat 3 meals.

The waiters were more than just a collection of male students. We were, in many respects, like a fraternity. We participated in intramural sports together, and we were concerned and involved in one another's welfare and lives. This was particularly true when it came to our girlfriends, most of which were Sardines. And so it was with me.

I managed to remain pretty much unattached until my senior year. The new year brought in many returning girls and a new crop of freshmen. Knowing that people are creatures of habit, and that SRD girls were no exception, I knew that I had to work fast to get the 16 girls who I wanted to sit at my two tables in a hurry because after that the girls' seating arrangement became set in concrete by their own choice.

One of the girls who gravitated to my table was a pretty freshman from Temple, Texas. Her name was Betty Clark and I decided I wanted to date her (though she would say she decided to date me). One day at dinner we were serving Mexican food and I managed to spill a plate of tamales in her lap and then offered to pick them up. She declined that offer but agreed to go out with me as reparation for my transgression. I was dating other girls at the time but soon found that I was spending more and more time with Betty. We would often double date with another waiter or waiters and their SRD girlfriends and though it has been 40 years, I can recall many of their names to this day.

Prior to my graduation, I asked Betty to marry me under the same magnolia tree that is still by the front entrance of SRD. Betty said "Yes," but following Texas traditions, I also asked her father if I could marry his daughter. He was on business out of state so I sent him a telegram. He called me and said "yes, provided you can maintain her in the manner to which she has become accustomed." I said I couldn't promise that but would promise to love and respect her. He agreed that was more important and said yes.

We were married in April of 1966. I was in the Air Force then and fulfilled another promise to Betty's parents; she received her bachelor's degree from the University of Arizona in 1968. We have spent the past 40 years happily married. We have four grown children and 6 grandchildren with the likely prospect that the grandchild count will grow.

We often think back to those days at the University of Texas and of SRD. These were institutions and these were people who shaped our lives forever.

—ALAN CHALFONT
Dishwasher/Waiter, 1961–1965
—BETTY CLARK CHALFONT
1964–1966

Food and Water

I started out as a dishwasher and "worked my way up" to waiter after a few months. I was a law student at the time at UT Austin.

I must say that, in regard to my employment at SRD, I enjoyed being a dishwasher more than being a waiter. You could wear jeans and tennis shoes and throw water and food at the other dishwashers back in the kitchen while, as a waiter, you had to dress up a little, wear a white jacket and you couldn't throw water or food at the women you were waiting on!

—JEFF WENTWORTH
Dishwasher/Waiter 1965–1966
State Senator, District 25

A Memorable Place

In 1945 my parents took me, a sixteen-year-old graduate of a small Northeast Texas high school, to enter the University of Texas. We pulled up in front of SRD, which loomed large to me since there were more residents of the dormitory than there were in my entire high school. I was, at once, awed, frightened, and very excited to be a college student.

My room was on the third floor and after all was unloaded and stashed in drawers and closets, my parents drove away, leaving me all alone to ponder my new life. Within minutes two seniors from down the hall came to my open door and invited me to walk over to the Triangle Grill at 27th and Guadalupe to have lunch with them. Lucy and Jeanne were harbingers of the friendliness that made SRD girls so special. Now, at 78 years, I continue to have lifelong friends first made within those walls.

My roommate, a Plan II student like me from a small town near Austin, brought more than her luggage to the dorm that afternoon. Her father owned a car dealership and her graduation present was a pale blue Buick convertible, one of the first to arrive after the war shortage.

She placed it in one of the small garages behind the dorm, which were no doubt made for Model A's. It was an attention getter for sure, especially with the returning vets from WW II.

There were concrete benches beneath the trees on the front lawn of SRD. It was on one of those benches that I practiced smoking, blowing the smoke wisps up my nostrils like Betty Davis in the movie *Now Voyager*. Once I mastered it without coughing, I felt sophisticated enough to smoke with the Dallas and Houston girls who hung out in "the smoker" on the first floor and who taught me to play bridge. Heady stuff, indeed!

I loved the meals at SRD. Except for breakfast, student waiters dressed in starched jackets served us on white cloth covered tables. We took turns at the head of the table and served plates, very ladylike. Our favorite dessert was Floating Island,* and to this day I have never tasted any quite as delicious as the ones at SRD

In the entrance hall of the dorm sat a table with a "sign out book" on it. There was a matron there to oversee where and with whom every girl was going. I'm sure the term "matron" is passé now and the 10:00 curfew for freshmen is gone as well. Nevertheless, I'll never forget one evening when our third floor matron was on duty, and my date and I were late returning from a steak fry near Mt. Bonnell. The reception was less than pleasant, and the icy tone of voice can still send chills down my spine!

Snow is rare in Austin, but one winter we got an inch or so, and my roommate and I were awakened one cold night to the sound of music. The Phi Gams from next door were serenading. Cole Porter's *In the Still of the Night* with a sublime tenor voice on a solo part was downright ethereal. We huddled together at the open window and clapped with frozen fingers. Serenades were fairly common at SRD, but this one is permanently etched in my memory.

How good it is to remember the many faces of the girls I knew at SRD. They remain, as they were then—young, full of life, and hopeful for the future.

—ANN MARABLE SPARKS PRIEST
1945–1947

*Floating Island is a dessert inspired by the French. It consists of delicate poached meringues floating on a pool of custard sauce, with a web of caramel drizzled over . . . thus the name. Floating Island can

be made up as individual desserts, or the meringues can be floated on a larger "sea" of custard sauce.

Residents Find Scottish Rite Desserts Irresistible

They are called CCBs, these chocolate crumble balls of vanilla ice cream, rolled in crushed Oreos and topped with a hot fudge sauce so thick you can eat it with a fork. They are the stuff of which dreams are made and the all-time favorite food at Scottish Rite Dormitory at the University of Texas.

Everybody piles down to the dining hall when CCBs are on the menu, says sophomore Lea Trimble.

If CCBs have a rival, it's the oatmeal cake, a moist chewy layer cloaked in a coat of brown sugar and butter, rough with coconut and pecans. Residents, present and past, sing its praises too.

"I liked the oatmeal cake better than the chocolate crumble balls," recalled Barbara Burrus Krege of Albuquerque, N.M., who lived at SRD almost 20 years ago. She has never forgotten this dessert. And her mother-in-law, Ida Mae Schkade of Giddings, wrote the *American-Statesman* seeking the recipe.

Since you seldom hear of dormitory food so good that alumni still talk about it 20 years later and actively seek its recipes, we decided to check out this kitchen. Not only did we find that SRD has some tempting goodies, but it can boast a cookbook, too. In December, *As you Like It*, rolled off the presses in honor of the dormitory's 60th year.

—KITTY CRIDER
Austin American-Statesman
©1983, excerpt reprinted
with permission

Room Service

Once during our second year in the dorm, Megan, my roommate, got tired of eating out on Sunday evenings, and she somehow managed to prepare an entire "gourmet" meal, right out of the microwave for us! Yummy chicken breasts with some sort of mushroom sauce, fresh veggies that she cooked with apple juice, a fresh salad—the works! That was my most memorable meal the entire time I lived there! I don't remember the entire menu, but it was certainly a testament to Meg's cooking skills.

—Genevra Davis Miller
1993–1996

Tornado!

During the summer session of 1972, we were eating dinner early one evening and noticed it had become almost as dark as night outside. From the below-ground dining room we didn't hear what was happening. After the meal, we went outside and discovered a twister had gone through the front lawn, made evident by the trees and branches that were down everywhere.

The tornado also hit close to the capitol building. We went there later that night to see the broken glass from the blown out windows all over the capital lawn. We felt very lucky that the twister didn't hit the dorm building, even though most of us were safe in the basement at the time.

—Anonymous
1972–1975

Holidays and Special Events

For Halloween, I remember drawing names and decorating the outside of our Pumpkin Pal's room. It was always fun to try and guess our Pal. We also had a Halloween costume contest. Everyone met in the Rec Room and showed off their costumes. Here are a few I remember: a Swiss Miss complete with the "Alp," a fried egg, and one hall coming as a centipede.

Another fun time was decorating for Dad's Day. Every year each hall came up with a theme for Dad's Day, and there would be a decorating contest. I remember my sophomore year (1977–78), 3rd Central picked a "football" theme. Luckily for us we had a couple of art majors. They created a backdrop of

Russell Erxleben kicking a field goal. The score board was seen behind him. They used gummed reinforcements to create the lights on the scoreboard.

As the Christmas season approached, the dorm became really "decked out." There was lots of garland and holiday décor. Each year we had a special Christmas dinner. Everyone got dressed up for the meal. Of course, we had CCBs, and then after dinner, one of the board members would play Christmas carols on the piano in the lobby. It was a lovely time.

I remember at least one year when we got up early one Saturday or Sunday morning, started on the 4th floor, singing carols, and then ended up in the dinning room for a special breakfast.

Once we had a '50s dance and everyone wore poodle skirts or rolled-up jeans. The waiters slicked back their hair, rolled up their T-shirt sleeves and donned leather jackets. Mrs. Evans and Mrs. Pruitt (the matrons) were decked out also. It was great to see them taking part ... Mrs. Potts may have even been in on it, too.

Thanks to SRD I have life-long friends. My memories of UT are tied to my memories of the dorm, its traditions, and the great girls who lived there. What a lucky group we were!
—ANNA HOLMGREN
1976–1980

Girls Deck Dorms in Holiday Décor

Deck the doors with boughs of holly. It is Christmas time and nothing could be more indicative of the season than the halls and lobbies of the girls' dorms.

Scottish Rite Dormitory is decorated in red and white. Red poinsettias and bells decorate the living room. A large white tree with red lights and ornaments is the center of attraction.

Upstairs, uniformity is scorned as each girl dons the Christmas spirit and tries to outdo her neighbor in decorating her dorm room door.

First place prizes in the four categories of religious, traditional, humorous, and original will be given after judging the doors next week.

The doors vary in décor and almost anything goes.

For the more ingenious and less ambitious there is the "do it yourself door." Mistletoe and several strips of colored wrapping paper have been hung on the door. At the bottom in scrambled letters is a note, "Merry Christmas."

Another door features the Wise Men scene made from different colored and textured fabrics. Black corduroy, grey wool and brown cotton camels seat the three Wise Men who are dressed in brightly colored clothes of satin, sequins, and rickrack.

Religious scenes of mosaic church windows, glittering angels, and nativity scenes covered with cellophane can be seen on many of the floors.

Girls in Kinsolving are working to meet the Open House deadline, 7:15 P.M. to 9:15 P.M. Wednesday.

The lobby area of each floor has a Christmas tree and many have made the area home-like by building fireplaces and hanging stockings.

One door reads, "Have a Real Old-Fashioned Christmas." Below the sign two dinosaurs marked (1,000,000 B.C.) hold a banner reading, "Season's Greeting."

Santa Claus is always popular, but each Santa has a different personality. Some have ruffled Kleenex beards, others are made of macaroni or have button eyes.

It is not difficult to get into the Christmas spirit by just walking down the halls of the dorms or by sitting in the lobbies.

—THE DAILY TEXAN
December 12, 1962
reprinted with permission

Egg Dye Dilemma

The Easter Eggstravaganza is an annual egg dying party that originated in my dorm room at SRD. This celebration is now in its 14th year and takes place wherever we happen to be living at the time.

Our first try at dying Easter eggs at SRD took place on first East, Room 17, with my freshman roommate Kathryn. We were so excited and thought we were ingenious for having a

Hot Pot in which to boil the eggs, food coloring, vinegar, and Dixie cups.

Not having considered that the cups were made with wax, we eagerly filled each with boiling water and food coloring. The cups did not begin to fail until we had filled them all and were getting ready to put in the eggs. When the melting was in full swing, there was a wave of color seeping everywhere including onto the carpet.

A cake pan from the closet stemmed the tide but the carpet was another story.

—AMIE STONE KING
1993–1997

The Secret

In the spring of 1946, I was only sixteen, and ready to begin my freshman year at UT, my father's alma mater. I had a confirmed room at SRD, but my best friend from North Dallas High School, Mary Strasburger, had been told there were no more vacancies and she would have to be on a waiting list. I was so disappointed.

Someone kept a secret, however, and on the day my family was helping me move into the dorm I found out that Mary had not only gotten a room, but she was my roommate! What joy! We fixed up our room with rose-colored Bates bedspreads* and matching curtains and settled down to our studies.

Mary went on to get her R.N. at Galveston and later became the mother of six! Her husband, Dr. Robert Cade, invented Gatorade at the University of Florida. I went on to get my B.S. in home economics, married, and became the mother of two. I pursued an early career in home furnishings, and a later one in nursing home therapeutic recreation.

Mary and I are still best friends sixty years later!

—MARJORIE KNIGHT WATSON
1946–1947

*In 1850, the Boston Industrialist Benjamin Bates formed Bates

Manufacturing Company, a textile mill in Lewiston, Maine. Bates of Maine became one of the great producers in the world of woven bedspreads. When the Bates Mill closed in 2001, a group of former employees formed Maine Heritage Weavers and continue to produce the Bates style bedspread.

On Top of the World

I moved into SRD the fall of 1957 and lived there for two years until May 1959. My roommate both years was a high school friend, Teddy Vanderwerth (now Boehm). Teddy and I both live in Brenham and have remained good friends our entire lives.

Both of my daughters, Rebecca Tate (Ehlert) (1982–1984) and Rachel Tate (Cangelosi) (1988–1989), also lived at SRD. In addition, one son-in-law, Chris Cangelosi, worked there as a waiter.

It was a fun, wonderful experience for a small town girl and my favorite memories were of the meals and formals. The food was the best I have ever had on a daily basis and served by those attentive waiters. I was really impressed by the decorations and food at the formals, too. Another luxury feature in those days was the laundry. You would leave all of your laundry out on Monday morning, and it would be returned to you in a day or two. We had to go down to the laundry to pick up our starched and ironed dresses. I thought we were living on top of the world!

—TWILA KIEKE TATE
1957–1959

No Room in the Inn

The day that Charles Whitman was shooting from the UT tower, I had an appointment with the dean of students, but was unable to get onto campus. Because I was accepted to UT late, finding housing was a problem. My family visited Kirby Hall which was a Methodist dorm at the time, and I thought, "Oh please don't make me live there!" Finally, we came to SRD. I begged and was put on a waiting list.

Ginger had also applied late, but SRD took all they could fit into their available space. We met when Ginger was living in the basement, and I was living in the maid's quarters. There were 11 girls in the "ward" as it was called. It was so crowded, but that helped us make friends really quickly. We each had a bed, a dresser and a rod on which to hang our clothes. In the maids' quarters the rooms were really nice and big, some of the best rooms in the dorm. After one semester, rooms on the main floors opened up and we moved to 1st East into a middle sunroom, the tiniest room in the dorm, with a trundle bed.

—Judy Lacks Gosslin
1966–1970
—Ginger Matthews Horton
1966–1970

The UT Tower

I was a mere high school junior when I first heard of the UT Tower. Some girls from my high school were down in Austin for the UIL competition. I think I was in the math and Latin competitions, and the contests were held in Batts Auditorium. One senior girl, who was headed for UT, said that while we had been at various UIL functions, she had sneaked off to meet a boy and they had kissed at the top of the UT Tower. I was shocked at her daring. As we drove out of town, she showed us the top of the Tower where she and the boy had been. "You can see everywhere in Austin from that tower," she said.

When I came down for college, my parents and I toured the campus on Saturday afternoon, since Mrs. McConnell wouldn't let us move into SRD yet. We went to the top of the tower. We entered a small elevator, rode to the top, and walked all around the four sides, looking out at what was then a very small Austin, Texas. It was beautiful, a little windy, and very sunny. Being that high gave me a new perspective on entering UT as a junior. I didn't feel any better, since we had been turned away from the dorm, but at least I had a bit more perspective.

During football season, the UT Band horn players would play spirited fanfares, as they stood on the Tower, under the clock, and faced down the South Mall. We walked to and from class, passing by the Tower, and the hours chimed every quarter hour.

In spring, in the English Building, as it was called then, we would be in class, with the windows wide open. We would pace ourselves through the lecture by the quarter hour chimes. At the 45-minute chime, most students would begin getting ready to leave the class, since the bell would ring in 5 minutes after that quarter hour chime. We had ten minutes between classes.

That year, I also found a refuge right behind the main building, in an outside, very pretty sitting area with concessions nearby, where I could sit underneath the north face of the Tower and study or read in between classes. That way I could be outside instead of in the Undergraduate Library, where I studied every night any way.

One day, in my 2:00 P.M. class, I heard that someone had jumped from the Tower that morning and landed near the concession area. I had missed the suicide by only a few minutes. I had just left before the young man had jumped. It was a desperate tragedy, but evidently not the first time something like that had happened.

We all had jokes about how we would jump from the Tower; we said it all the time, but no one I ever knew actually jumped.

Later, as a graduate student, when I got access to the library's stacks, I would ride up the little bitty elevator with the grilled screen to whatever floor, usually the 12th, I needed to find the books I wanted. I would often sit in one of the window study carrels and look out.

I didn't stay long in the Tower's stacks because the light was dim, it was crowded with cases of books, the ceilings were low, and the concrete floors made a spooky sound. Plus I never knew who might get off the elevator.

Anybody might be in the stacks—including one of our professors. That was always a jolt. Seeing a professor outside of class, and having to speak to the professor, or figure out how to avoid speaking, if it was a shy moment.

The Whitman Incident

In the summer of 1966, my roommate Gay and I had driven down to Austin in her VW beetle to look for an apartment for the fall semester. We had decided not to live in SRD that year, although I loved SRD and didn't really want to move out. However, my boyfriend Gene Raborn and I had broken up, and I didn't really want to be back at SRD, since that had many "waiter" memories. Ah-h-h-h-h, youth. So many decisions made so whimsically for flimsy reasons. Anyway, we were driving by the South Mall at about noon, if I remember correctly. We saw some very obvious things going on, but couldn't figure out what was up. "Gay!" I said. "There's someone in the Tower. Park the car! Let's go see what's happening!"

She did immediately, because she had a Beetle, and because we could park in practically no space. We hopped out of the car and began running by the fountain and up the South Mall on the Batts-Mezes side. Someone, a young man, crouched and hiding behind the tree, yelled at us, "Get down! There's a guy in the Tower and he's shooting!"

We just laughed, because that was the joke. Someone was always going to do something deadly from the Tower—jump and commit suicide, or start shooting. It was a college joke. Then the guy cursed at us, "Goddamit, girls! Get down! He's shooting!"

I looked up to see a figure facing to the west side toward the Drag. I could see a gun and a white shirt. "Gay!! Let's get into Batts. We can see from those windows!" As we ran up the sidewalk, I could see a woman hunkered down and hiding behind the flag pole in front of what was the WMOB (West Mall Office Building). There was a guy hiding behind the bushes on Inner Campus Drive. Several other people were crouched behind things. I don't remember seeing anyone that I thought at the moment might be dead. We were still, like kids, running because of the excitement. We had no idea of the unfolding tragedy.

So we sprinted into Batts and climbed the stairs to the first floor. We darted into the classroom, threaded our way through the desks, and looked out at the Tower through the open wide, big windows in Batts, trying to get a glimpse of the action. Just as we got to the windows to look out, a young, dark-haired, uniformed UT policeman came screaming into the room, "Get away from those windows! Get out of this room! Get down in the basement! NOW!!" So, because he was a policeman, Gay and I reluctantly went back down the stairs we had just sprinted up, and down another flight into the basement of Batts.

As we got downstairs, an entire class of high school students emerged from the Batts Auditorium in the basement. They were there for Freshman Orientation. As the news spread through the dozens of students emerging, I heard one girl say in a loud lament, "OH, NO!! Now my mother will NEVER let me come here!!"

We were in that basement for hours—closed off, isolated, and milling. No lunch, no drinks, no word. Finally, when the drama was over, we were allowed to leave. I remember it being near supper, but my sense of time may be off. It may have been mid- to late-afternoon.

We went back down to Gay's car, and drove to my brother's, where we were staying with him and his young wife. The news that evening was grim. The phone lines were jammed. I tried to call home over and over to let my parents know I was OK. I don't think I got through to them until about 11 P.M.

I finally broke down and called my ex-boyfriend Gene, who was in summer school finishing up his degree for graduation that August. I knew two of his roommates—Grover McMains and Turner Bratton—were ambulance drivers. They had also been waiters at SRD. He told me that both of them were working and had brought several people into the hospitals who were already dead.

He also had the news that Lana had been shot in the shoulder. She was a music major who lived in SRD and was a good friend of Gay's. Gay was also a music major. Lana had been shopping on the Drag and had just come out of the store when she was shot. She may have been standing looking in a window of the next store. That night the entire city of Austin was in shock and mourning. We could hardly sleep and kept talking and talking about our near miss. We never spoke of our foolhardiness, only our near miss.

The next day, Gay and I went home to Longview, without looking for an apartment at all. About a week later, around July 4th it seems to me, Grover called me. He and Abner Kestler, also a waiter at SRD, were managers of the Rio Grande Apartments. They had saved a two-bedroom apartment for us, and we could have it with our deposit. So in September, Gay Correll, Nita Schweatmann, Trish Carlson, and I (all of us Baptist girls!) lived in a two-bedroom apartment with a red rug. By the end of the spring semester, I was moving back into SRD to finish my graduate degree, Nita was getting married and moving to a small house on Bonnie Lane, Trish was moving back home, and Gay was going to be Nita's roommate. That year, there were rumblings of the SDS being in Austin, and the Vietnam war protests were beginning.

This is what I don't know: I don't know who the young man was that first yelled at us. I don't know what happened to the young UT policeman who shooed us down into the Batts basement. I don't know if the high school girl ever got to come to UT with her mother's permission.

Gay finished her music degree, eventually married a lawyer, and has lived forever in El Paso. Nita got married to Ray, who was in the Navy ROTC, then got divorced. Trish became a medical records librarian. Lana recovered from her gunshot wounds. I saw her later with what looked like blue shrapnel marks still left in her shoulder. Abner Kestler went to Vietnam, survived, married, and lived in Austin and San Antonio, before I lost contact. Grover McMains, an Air Force ROTC, became a pilot for the university. Turner Bratton never did get into medical school, but became a nurse, I think. Gene Raborn worked for Brown and Root in Africa and Kuwait, and has disappeared.

This is what I do know. I moved back into a trundle on Second East for the summer of 1967, the summer of the student riots in Detroit. I graduated with my masters. I taught for six years, came back to get my Ph.D., and twelve years after the summer of the Whitman shootings, I graduated. I walked up the stairs on the South Mall in the evening shadows and stood facing south under the Tower, while the president of the university put my Ph.D. hood over my head. I walked back down the stairs under the Tower, in the doctoral procession.

My entire family, including the married brother now with his two children, sat in the East Gallery, just across Inner Campus drive, right up from the flung-wide-open windows of Batts.

Sic transit mundi.

—JANE ARCHER FEINSTEIN
1964–1966, 1967

Jerry Moore, former SRD resident, was employed in the BEOB as the head of job placement for the business school. She recalls crawling out of her office and down the hall as the windows of her office were shot out by crossfire during the event.

And the Winner Is ...

Pajama parties were always fun, but one of the most anticipated events of the early 1960s was Academy Awards night. Each wing would rent a television for the night, order pizza, and then ooh and ah over our favorite movie stars, what they were wearing, and who they were with.

—MARY MARGARET (BATES) DURHAM
1959–1961

Waiters Give Corsage Prize

Bunny Finnell was dubbed, "The Girl Who Has to Do the Most to Become Beautiful by 8:00 P.M." Prior to Scottish Rite Dormitory's spring formal Friday night, Bunny was presented with an onion-and-carrot corsage by Joe Foster and Hugh Ross, SRD waiters.

The meal before the formal is the only one during the year when girls are permitted to wear jeans and pin-curls to the dining room.

Chairmen of the dance were Pat Paget, Lynn Jones, Betty Hart, Nancy Haston, La Donna Taylor, Marilyn Barron, Peggy Hemley, and Sally Spencer. Nancy Moon and Jan McKenzie did mural work. Joan McKenzie was in charge of the floor show.

—*THE DAILY TEXAN*
March 11, 1956
reprinted with permission

History, Furniture, and Character

I have so many fond memories of dorm life at SRD. I went pot luck and got a great roommate, Brittney Byerly. We lived on 3rd East in a sunroom. A few of my favorite things that our fabulous dinning hall provided, besides the cute wait staff, were CCB's (of course!!), chicken finger day, and the frozen yogurt ... which all contributed to the famous "freshman 15." Being an interior design major, I loved living in the historic dorm: the beautiful details, antique furniture, the history, the character ... even the faint smell of mildew and the ghosts. I was always a little scared any time I had to go up to the 4th floor storage, to pass by the empty dining hall at night, or come in after hours through the boiler room.

Overall, living at SRD was an experience that I would not trade for anything. It was a wonderful place to call home my first year away. I will always remember waking up in our beautiful sunny room, walking the grounds to and from class, hanging out in the common room, lying out by the pool, and most of all the friends that I made.

—LAURA KING MILLER
1997–1998

Elevators, Phones, and Don't Go There!

How many of you remember that the elevator would get stuck if you opened that folding door too many times? Sometimes it got stuck for an unknown reason. I was working as RA one night, and my shift was just about over when I heard my name being called, "Anna, Anna ..." I kept looking but no one was around. Finally I heard, "Anna, it's Sarah (Holcomb). I'll be late to replace you ... the elevator is stuck!"

Before there were cell phones, everyone would get extra long cords for their phones and put them in the hall while we watched TV in the "smokers" at the east and west ends of the floor. Everyone got pretty good at recognizing the ring and could tell whose phone was ringing.

Someone on *The Daily Texan* staff decided to do an article on SRD and the décor of the living room. Everyone was anxiously awaiting the article, and then it was published. Boy, you've never seen such a riled up group of young women. Basically the article knocked the dorm and its furnishings. I believe there was something about the "silly stilted velvet valances" . . . or something like that. We were really upset that they would come in and in today's slang . . . "dis" our home.*

—ANNA HOLMGREN
1976–1980

When *The Daily Texan* printed the unflattering article about SRD, then residents, Donna (Dunn) Gross, Lu Anne (Wisrodt) Freemen, and Kathy Keils, wrote letters to the editor vehemently disagreeing with the article which were printed in the paper.

Driving School

In the spring of 1946 I was sixteen, a freshman at UT, and living at SRD. This was before the days of driver's education, and I didn't yet have my driver's license. My dad had patiently let me drive with him a few times in a local cemetery in Dallas, but I still needed more practice. I got that help, generously given, from a new friend at SRD, Mary Lou Babel. I'll always remember her patience (and courage) in riding with me in her car and letting me drive around the SRD neighborhood.

That summer I went home and surprised my family by getting my license! Subsequently, I taught my SRD roommate, Mary Strasburger, how to drive.

I regret I have lost touch with Mary Lou but will never forget her. As a postscript, I still drive and have an excellent driving record.

—MARJORIE KNIGHT WATSON
1946–1947

Bing Crosby

In the fall semester of 1975, Mary Frances Crosby, Bing Crosby's daughter, lived at SRD. One Friday night while I was studying for a big exam I heard someone say that Bing had come by the dorm to pick up his daughter. Later that evening

I was talking to my mother on the phone and told her about Bing coming by the dorm. She told me to STOP STUDYING and sit by that front door until they returned! This really surprised me since my grades weren't too hot, and she was always happy to hear that I was studying. Following her orders, I sat by the front door for several hours waiting for them to return, but it didn't happen that night. I later found out that she had returned to the dorm the following day, having spent the night with her father at a hotel. It was my one and only chance to see Bing Crosby and I missed it!

—ANONYMOUS
1972–1975

Current Thoughts About SRD

Amie: What do you like most about the dorm?

Jennifer: I love how everyone is so nice to each other and just the girly atmosphere, hall decorations and cookies in the lobby area. Seeing girls who can roll out of bed and be okay with how they look.

And just being girls, like the other night my friend and I were studying in the Rec Room and it was like 3:00 in the morning and we just started dancing. If anyone had seen us, it would have just been crazy, but it was so much fun.

I've talked to dads who had dates with girls here, and they say it like it was a big accomplishment. "Yeah, I've picked up girls there!"

I like how old it is. I've talked to some people and they say, "Yes, I lived there in the olden days." It has a lot of history.

My roommate bought a shower radio that now graces the bathroom on 2nd East.

Amie: Anything else you'd like to add?

Jennifer: I'm afraid of the 5th floor study room.

Kicking boys out at 12:00 A.M. I think that's funny—the walk of guys leaving SRD at midnight.

The frozen yogurt is #1 on all of our lists!

—JENNIFER SEAMARK
2006–present

204 ~ It's a Sardine's Life for Me

A Lesson by Candlelight

My mother attended Texas Woman's University during World War II. My childhood was filled with tales of my mother's antics in the dorm at TWU, in her effort to keep her heart light and away from the war. I longed to grow up and become my mother.

So when I arrived on the steps of Scottish Rite in the fall of 1970, I said quietly and to my heart-of-hearts, "This dorm is mine!"

Quickly adjusting to college life I was soon into short-sheeting beds, putting toothpaste on phone receivers, and pouring buckets of cold water over the heads of my freshman floor mates during showers. Eventually, though, everyone came to expect this of me, and the thrill began to pale.

One night in November word spread like wildfire that the boys from Jester were on their way through campus, would by-pass Kinsolving, and had a final destination of SRD. I was electrified at the revival of my mother's college tradition: a real panty raid! Immediately I sought out my best pair of panties, opened my dorm room window, and to the delight of all the freshmen on Fourth Floor threw them out into the vast darkness below.

The next morning I was hauled into Mrs. McConnell's office. Someone had found my panties in the bushes with my name clearly stamped in the elastic. I had no choice at this point but to lay low.

Fall turned into winter, and winter into spring. With graduation upon us and my moving out of the dorm for my sophomore year, I had to do something to create a final memory of dorm life to tell my future children. But what?

It came to me during a conversation with Sherry, our beloved floor advisor. She had always wanted a "candlelight" on her floor. A candlelight, you will remember, is when you form a circle of floor mates and pass around a candle: once for luck, twice for dropped, three times for pinned, and four times for engaged. Someone blows out the candle on the appropriate circle. All of it is anonymous, and no one knows who is dropped, pinned, or engaged until that girl blows out the candle.

We were all freshmen on the Fourth Floor. There had never

been a candlelight on the Fourth Floor, that anyone could re-member. Well, "Why not?." I asked myself. Sherry wants a candlelight. I need a memory. And the plan was born.

That afternoon I anonymously slipped a note under Sherry's door, requesting the candlelight. In an instant the word was out! The whole dorm buzzed with excitement at the prospect. WHO was it! By that night Sherry's room was so crowded it was standing room only.

With much ceremony the candle began its journey. Once for luck. Twice around for dropped. And no one blew it out! As it began a third circling everyone was looking at everyone. A freshman, pinned? Sherry, our own Miss Jean Brodie, was clearly nervous. Under her nose? Who? I thought to myself, "This isn't working! You must DO something! But what?" I couldn't blow out the candle! I hadn't had a date in months, let alone be pinned by a fraternity guy.

As the flame began its fourth and last circle, Sherry was more than concerned. Someone was engaged. And this couldn't happen to a freshman girl on her watch. I was miserable.

When the fourth circling ended and no one had blown out the candle, the silence was deafening. We just sat there, for a long time. And then, all eyes were on me. Who else would have faked a candlelight but me?

"Would you believe I'm married?" I said sheepishly, taking the candle and blowing it out. Sherry smiled that great smile, then hurled pillow upon pillow at me, thereby bridging the moment and saving me from endless humiliation.

Life lesson learned.

—Anonymous

FAREWELL

Farewell to days and pleasant ways
Of happy Sardee's clime;
To friends so true and good times, too,
That were so fair and fine!
The years roll on. Old times are gone,
Supplanted by the new.
And when I see the change, ah me,
It makes me feel quite blue!
And yet 'tis true, the friends we knew,
So dear to you and me,
Though far away, shall live for aye
In golden memory!
'Tis sweet to know, as on we go,
This truth which is divine;
We'll ne'er forget the friends we've met
In Sardee that is mine!"

—The Sardine
Volume 9, May 1931

Scottish Rite Dormitory.

J. F. Newton visit, 1927.

Scottish Rite Dormitory 1946.

Scottish Rite Dormitory 1946.

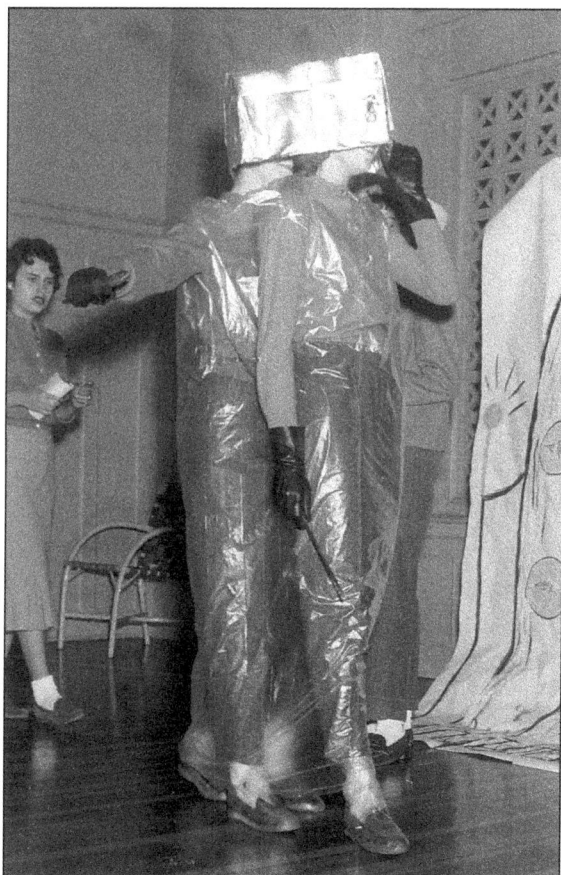

Pajama Party Skit 1957.

Pajama Party 1959 or 1960.

Pajama Party 1960.

Waiter Skit Mid-1960s.

Formal 1960s.

Hanging out in 1973.

Dube's dolls in 1976

Girl with SRD Armband,1922

Spring Formal 1976.

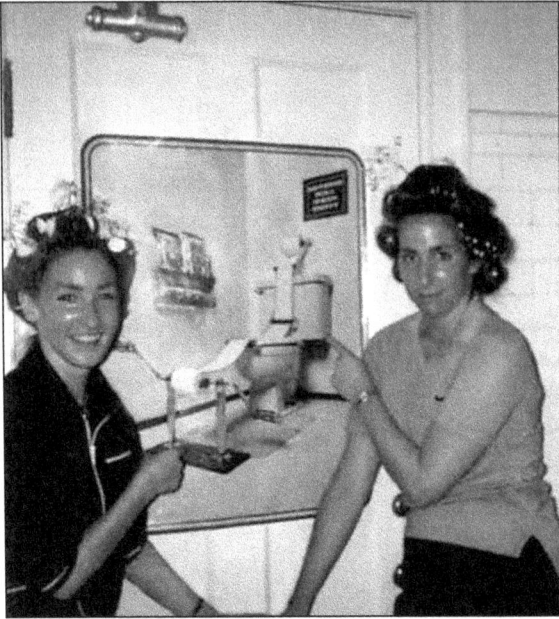

1980s.

Academy Awards 1981.

Hanging out in the Living Room 1980s.

Waiters in 1980.

Bathing Beauties 1981.

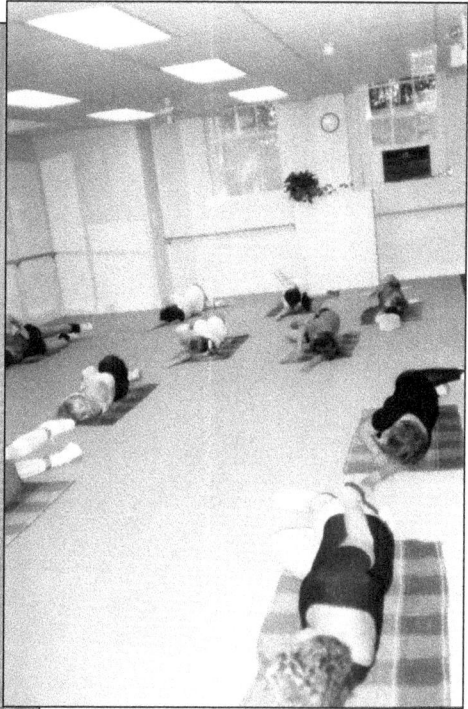

Aerobics Class 1987.

Recognition Dinner 1987.

Christmas Party 1990.

CCB Riot 1991.

Bar-B-Que Picnic 1992.

Valentines 1997.

Holiday Dinner Flutes 1996.

Graduation 2004

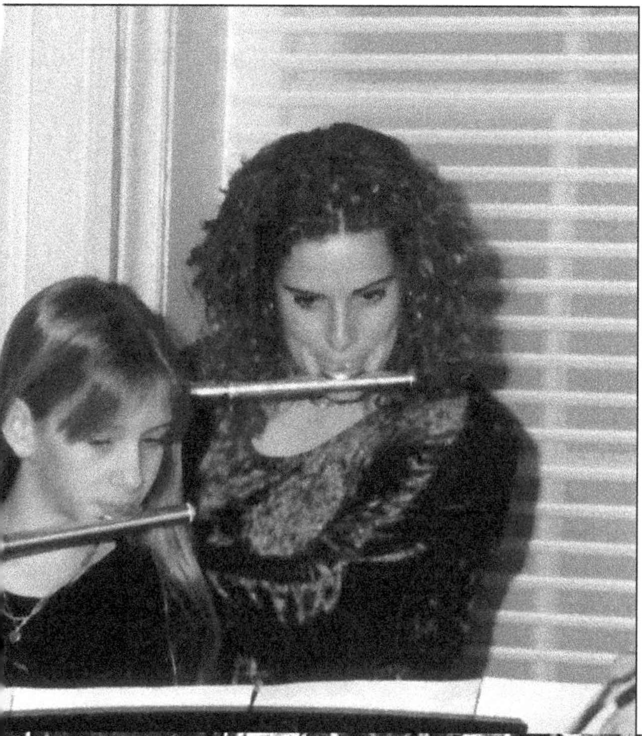

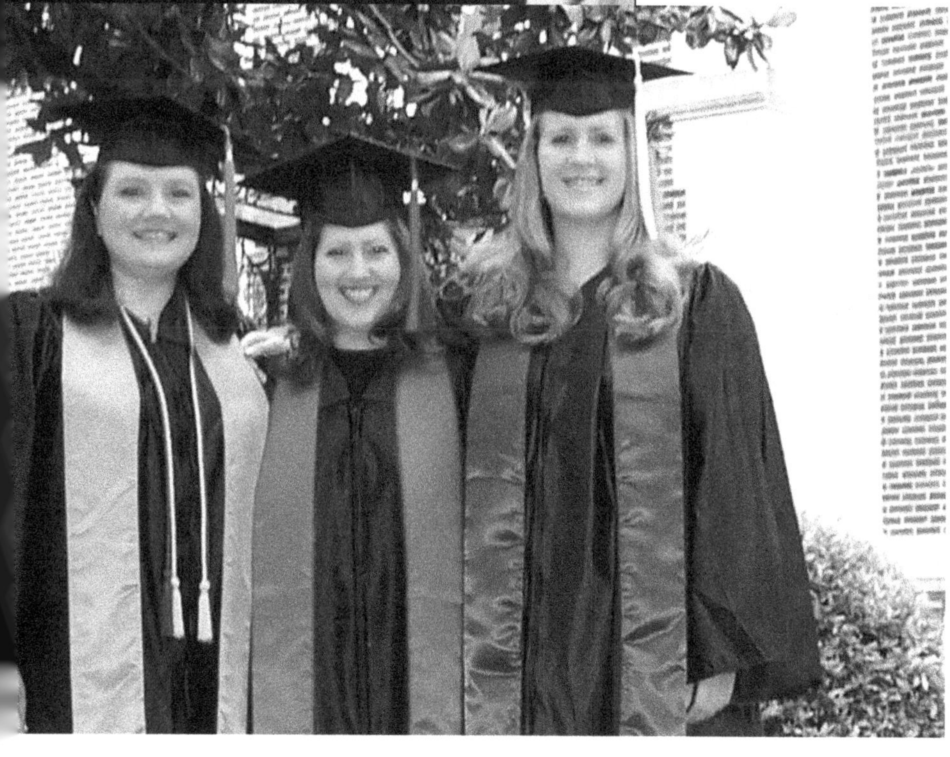

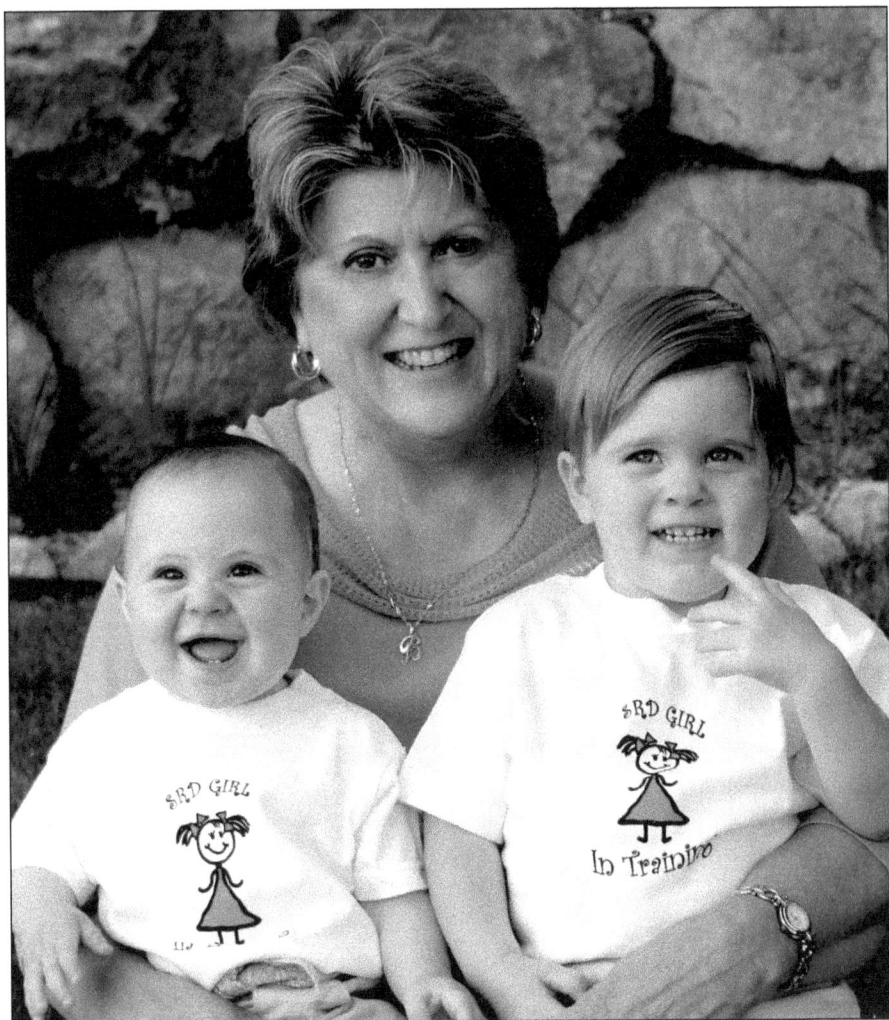

The Next Generation.

Afterword

My first thought for the title of this memoir was *Girls Will Be Girls* because it is clear from these stories spanning nine decades that young women have changed little in their desire for the comforts of home and a safe environment from which to stretch their wings and fly.

Scottish Rite Dorm is a safe haven. A place where loving people provide wonderful food, rescue from car trouble, change sheets, clean rooms, entertain with holiday parties, listen to woes, protect from ghosts, whether real or imagined and support with sincere concern. As my four-year old daughter Marillah replied when asked to sum up SRD, "It's a place for girls." How right she is.

Thank you to the past, present, and future staff of SRD. Because of you, as Janice Gregory said, "Forever it is a special place."

www.ingramcontent.com/pod-product-compliance
Lightning Source LLC
Chambersburg PA
CBHW060045100426
42742CB00014B/2707